CW01391113

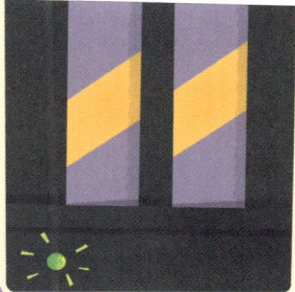

100 WAYS TO SAVE THE PLANET

100 WAYS TO SAVE THE PLANET

EVERYTHING YOU NEED TO KNOW TO BECOME A GREEN SUPERHERO

TOM JORDAN & JOSHUA RICE

Button
BOOKS

CONTENTS

Fill your old boots – see **82**

Houseplant heaven – see **57**

Think like a penguin – see **71-75**

Turn leaves into compost – see **31**

ABOUT THIS BOOK

Saving the planet sounds a bit dramatic. After all, Earth existed for billions of years before humans came along, and will be around for a few billion more. Really, we're talking about saving **nature**. Wide-open wildernesses and endless oceans; garden grass and trickling streams; ants and elephants; butterflies and bats; blue whales and red squirrels; migrating birds and hibernating bears; thousand-year-old trees and springtime saplings; snowdrops and sunflowers; simple patterns and complex ecosystems. All the things that make Earth a marvellous, mysterious, bountiful place for humans to live.

Nature's wonders are all around us, growing and flourishing in many places. But they're also under strain from human activity: the space we take up, the energy we use, the things we consume and throw away, the pollution we produce. You've probably heard a lot about these problems, and the stories can be worrying. You might also have felt like you wish you could do something to help, but that you're only one person and how can *you* possibly make much difference? That's *one* way of looking at things. But here's another. Think of all the action stories you've read or watched. In times of trouble, the ***best*** characters emerge – the **Superheroes**. And now you've picked up this book, you're about to become part of a new generation of **Green Superheroes**, battling together to restore the natural balance of the planet.

The book contains 100 activities to help you go on a remarkable journey from ordinary kid to the **Ultimate Green Superhero**. They may *seem* random, and apart from starting with **1** and finishing with **100**, you can do them in any order. You might not be able to do every one, you may already do some of the actions, or they might inspire you to do something different. But the more you do, the more you'll begin to notice the connections. Like ecosystems in nature, *everything* is linked, and every action you take will have a wider impact on the world around you.

For example: making a pond in your garden doesn't just help frogs. There'll be more insects too, laying eggs in the water. More insects means more things that love to eat insects, like birds and mini-mammals. More creatures means more seed spreading, on fur and in droppings. More seed spreading means more flowers growing, which means more pollinators like bees and butterflies in your garden, and more flowers flourishing in neighbouring gardens too. And so on and so on. One action leading to dozens of benefits for nature. Or, a simple act like learning about labels on products could mean that your house produces less waste, cuts down its food air miles, saves water, and protects marine life *and* orangutans.

And every time *you* do something positive for nature, some of the energy and magic *you* generate will rub off on *other* people – and *their* positivity will grow too. Your neighbours, friends, family, and school. Lots of the activities will help you to do this – sometimes in little ways, sometimes in big ways, but often in ways you might not even notice.

Many activities are about solving problems, but others are about something just as important – **enjoying nature**. Taking time to go exploring, or investigating, or playing, or discovering, or adventuring will refill your Green Superhero energy levels, and remind you what a wonderful, wild world it is that you're trying to protect. And while most of this book is about *doing*, sometimes it's worth pausing to *think:* about the past, about the future; about new ideas from the depths of your imagination, and ancient stories hidden in plain sight; about worms and the world; about swifts and the stars... and about seeing and doing things *differently*.

Finally, as you go, keep this in mind: from little things, big things grow – and from many small habits, big changes happen. And *always* remember that you're not on this journey alone. You're part of a movement of millions of Green Superheroes across the world. The future is yours. So be bold, be brave, be adventurous, be strong, be kind, be creative, be caring. **Be a Green Superhero**.

And, most importantly... have fun!

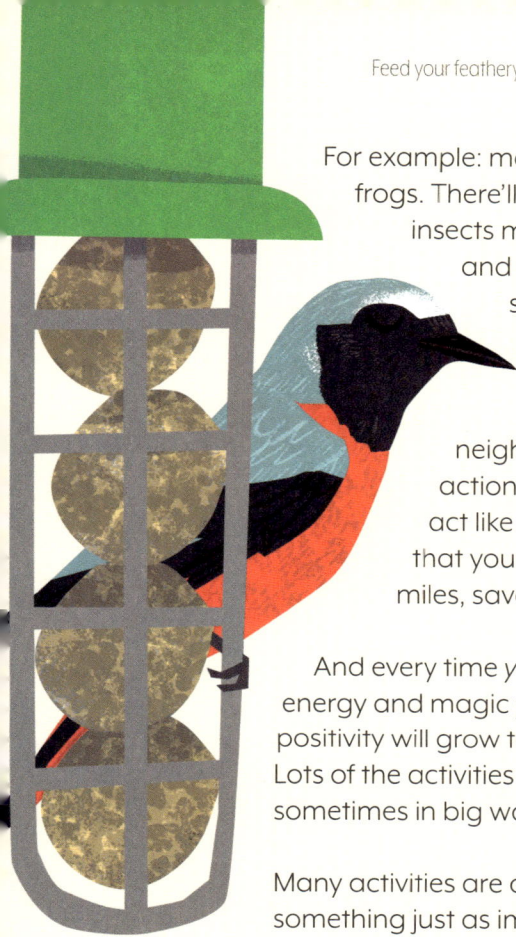

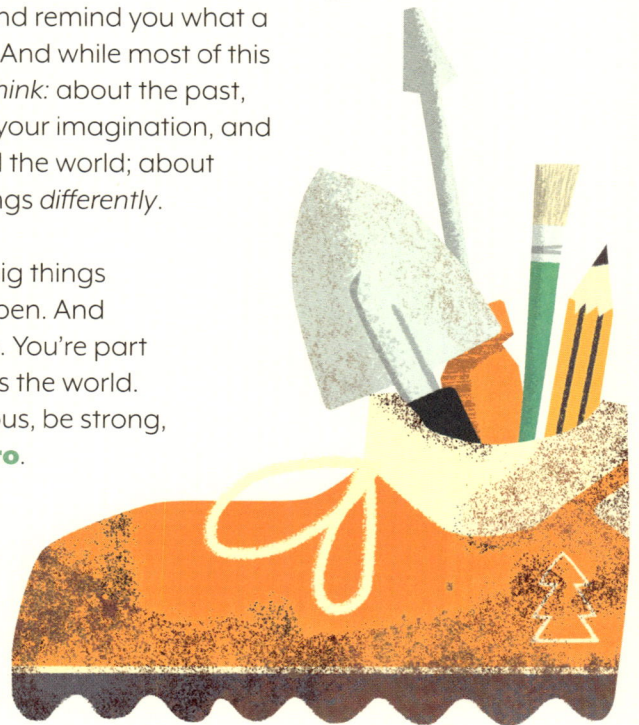

1
YOUR GREEN SUPERHERO FOOTPRINT

Draw around your foot (either one) on a piece of paper, then stick it somewhere you can see it every day. This is your **Green Superhero Footprint**. As you work your way through this book, colour a bit (1 per cent) of your footprint green each time you complete an activity. Over the next year, this is your challenge: can you turn your footprint completely green, and become the **Ultimate Green Superhero**? You can add your first bit of colour by working out a different kind of footprint: **your carbon footprint**. This is an estimate of all the greenhouse gases you create in your daily life, from the energy you use at home to the way you travel, and the things you buy and eat. Nature organizations like the WWF have carbon footprint calculators on their websites. Have a go at filling in one of their surveys, and make a note of your score. Then, when you complete your **Green Superhero Footprint**, work it out again. You'll see that all the amazing things you've done have made a big difference.

2 EDGE TOWARDS VEG

There's a really simple way to start cutting down your carbon footprint straight away: **eat less meat**. The meat and dairy industry produces nearly 15 per cent of the world's manmade greenhouse gas emissions, due to methane emitted by livestock (think windy cows!), the growth of animal feed, transport and the deforestation of precious places like the Amazon to create more land for pasture.

However, if you love to munch on a bacon butty, burger or hot dog, the idea of giving up meat completely might feel too difficult. In that case, try a small change to start with: make **one day a week in your household meat-free**. If you only eat meat four days a week, cut it down to three. And if you already have a meat-free diet, invite a non-vegetarian friend round for a delicious dinner, then ask them to try having it at home instead of a meat meal next week (and hopefully every week after too). For an extra challenge, try **keeping a dairy diary** for one week, making a note of all the meat and dairy you consume. Then make the next week completely meat-and-dairy-free, and keep a diary of that too. Compare notes and see if there are any changes you'd be willing to make permanently.

Did you know? Some of the largest and strongest wild animals in the world, including elephants, hippos, rhinos and mountain gorillas, are herbivores – meaning they don't eat meat.

WHAT ARE GREENHOUSE GASES?

Greenhouse gases, such as carbon dioxide and methane, help insulate the Earth by forming a kind of invisible blanket in the atmosphere that traps heat from the sun. We need them to make our planet liveable – but humans are currently producing *too much* of them, which is making the planet too hot. The main causes are the use of fossil fuels such as gas, oil and coal, and farming and deforestation.

There are lots of ideas for eating and growing veg in this book – see **14**, **17** & **45**.

3 BECOME AN EXPERT

Nature experts are impressive people. They know so many interesting facts about animals, plants and ecosystems that it can seem mind-blowing. But everyone who's an expert today started out somewhere. In fact, they once knew *nothing* about the subject they now know *everything* about – so there's no reason why *you* can't become an expert too! Here are two ways to begin your journey to becoming a nature expert.

PART ONE

Think of a topic you're interested in discovering more about, and find an inspiring expert to learn from. The coolest experts are the ones that are passionate about their subject. Looking in the nature section of your local library or bookshop, and searching for wildlife programmes or videos, are good ways to get started. Once you find an expert you like, you'll be amazed at how much you can discover from them. You might well find yourself disappearing down an **expert rabbit hole** – where one interesting thing you discover makes you want to find out more about something else, which leads to another discovery, and another, and another... and before you know it, and without realizing it, *you're* an expert too!

PART TWO

Complete the 'Learn Your...' activities in this book: Learn Your Birds, Learn Your Trees, Learn Your Mammals, Learn Your Minibeasts. You'll quickly go from knowing not much to knowing a lot in just a few days, and you'll be well on your way to becoming **the world's newest expert**!

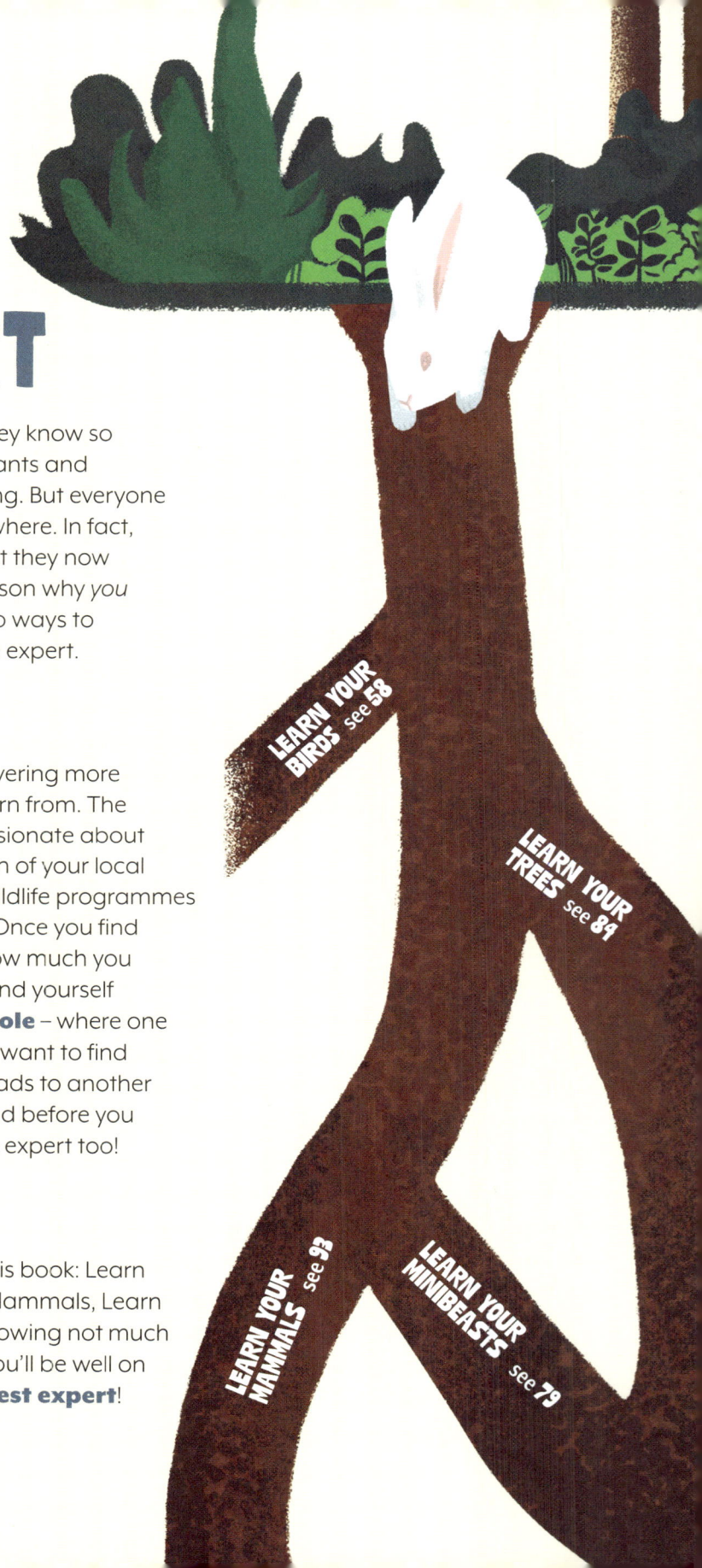

LEARN YOUR BIRDS see 58

LEARN YOUR TREES see 84

LEARN YOUR MAMMALS see 93

LEARN YOUR MINIBEASTS see 79

4 YEAR OF THE BIRD

Nice big drink

Tasty snacks

Notepad & pencil

Bird-spotting guide

This is a **two-part birdwatching challenge**, to try one year apart. The first time to do it is right away, before you begin transforming your patch into a wildlife wonderland. Pick a spot inside by a window, with a good view of your garden or the area you look out on to, and get comfortable (snacks and drinks are essential!). Watch for one hour, making note of the different types of birds that appear, and how many of them you see. Then, add up everything you've spotted, and keep your notes in a safe place. Over the next 12 months, do as many of the garden activities in this book as you can. Exactly one year later, retake the birdwatch (remember the snacks!). Compare your results from the first survey, and see how much difference all of your efforts have made.

If you enjoyed this activity, there are local, national and international bird surveys you can take part in, such as the RSPB Big Garden Birdwatch in the UK, or the Great Backyard Bird Count, which adds together individual counts from all over the world.

Binoculars (if you have a pair)

Camera or phone

WAYS OF COUNTING

There are different approaches you can take to your notes. You can record *every* bird you see, but you may end up counting the same bird more than once. Alternatively, you can make a note of the largest number of a bird species that you see *at the same time*. For example, if you see one crow, mark a '1' next to 'Crow' in your notebook. Later, if you see three crows together, update your tally to '3'. If you then see another crow on its own, or a pair, your tally remains at 3. But if you see *five* together later, then update it to 5. That way you know that there are *at least* five crows that come into your garden.

Ideas to boost your bird count – see **6, 7, 8, 34, 59, 60** & **78**.

5
STORE WHEN IT POURS

Camels have perfected the art of storing water. Not in their humps, which are actually fat reserves, but by drinking more than 26 gallons (100 litres) at a time when they find water, which is stored in their bloodstream to see them through the dry times. A barrel that connects to a drainpipe from your roof is a great way to **think like a camel** and store water when it rains, to use in your garden when it doesn't. You can use the water you collect for all kinds of useful tasks, from plant watering to giving wildlife a drink (see **7**), and even filling your pond (see **8**).

How to collect rainwater

Water butts are available to buy from garden or hardware shops, and can typically store around 53 gallons/200 litres (that's at least 15 teeth cleans – see **13**). They help conserve resources in hot weather, and provide a good natural water source. You could always ask for one for a Birthday Bonus – see **41**).

6
LET THE GRASS GROW

Short grass in your garden may look neat, but it's soooo dull for wildlife! Letting a patch of lawn grow long during spring and summer does wonders for biodiversity. First come the florets – the swaying sea of green develops a colourful hue as flowers appear. Then come the butterflies and the bees, attracted by the pollen, closely followed by a cast of small mammals and amphibians (especially if you've built a pond nearby), who will love making a home in your wild garden.

No-mow hair grow

For extra fun, let your hair grow for as long as you let your grass grow, and keep an eye out for fellow long-haired no-mowers!

7 WILDLIFE WATERING HOLES

Watering holes are the best locations to spot wildlife on an exotic safari – animals come from far and wide across the savannahs to drink and bathe at these amazing oases. And you can create your own backyard safari watering holes too – all you need is a well-positioned container and a few extras. Choose one (or all) of these options, keep it topped up with water, and the wildlife will soon appear.

BUTTERFLY OASIS

Find a shallow bowl or saucer. Add sand or soil to soak up some of the water, plus stones that poke out of the top for landing on. Place near butterfly-friendly flowers.

MAMMAL LAGOON

A simple shallow bowl or saucer will do. No stones are needed. Place near hedges or shrubs to provide good cover for small mammals.

BIRD BATH

Use a shallow, wide dish, bowl or even a bin lid. Include a rock or stones for birds to perch on. Raise it off the floor to avoid cat ambushes.

Wildlife watering holes make great locations for filming a nature documentary – see **22**.

8
MAKE A MAGIC POND

Ponds truly are magical – if you make one, it won't be long before all kinds of creatures appear in your garden. A **wildlife pond** is one of the best ways to boost nature as it creates a whole new ecosystem. Below are the basic steps you need to make a magical pond. It can be as large or as small as space allows. Alternatively, if you don't have enough room to dig, you can make a cool mini-pond out of a bucket or washing-up bowl – see **83**.

Pond liner

Layer of sand (2in/5cm)

STEP 1

Choose a spot, ideally one that gets both sunshine and shade, and mark out the size and shape of your pond. Make sure the amount of lining you have is twice as big as the perimeter of the shape you mark, as it will need to cover the sides of the hole you dig too.

STEP 2

Grab your spade and **get digging**! How deep you can go depends on obstacles you might encounter in the ground, like tree roots or rock, but the important thing is to make sure there are some shallow, sloping parts so it's easier for wildlife to get in and out of the pond. As a bonus, you can use the soil you dig up to fill new flower beds or plant pots.

STEP 3

Make sure the top of the hole is **level**, so that the water doesn't flow out of one side when you fill it up. Get your plank of wood and lay it across from one side of the pond to the other. Place a spirit level on top of the plank. When it looks like this, it's level.

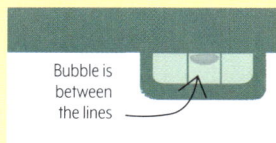

Bubble is between the lines

Move the plank around and repeat the process at different angles.

STEP 4

Pick out any sharp stones or sticks from the bottom and side of the pond, so that your lining won't get damaged. Next, spread a 2in (5cm) layer of **sand** across the bottom of the hole. This gives your lining a good cushion, and helps to stop seeds and shoots trying to grow underneath the pond. There's one more bit of digging to do – you'll need a small dip a few centimetres deep around the edges of your hole to tuck the liner into.

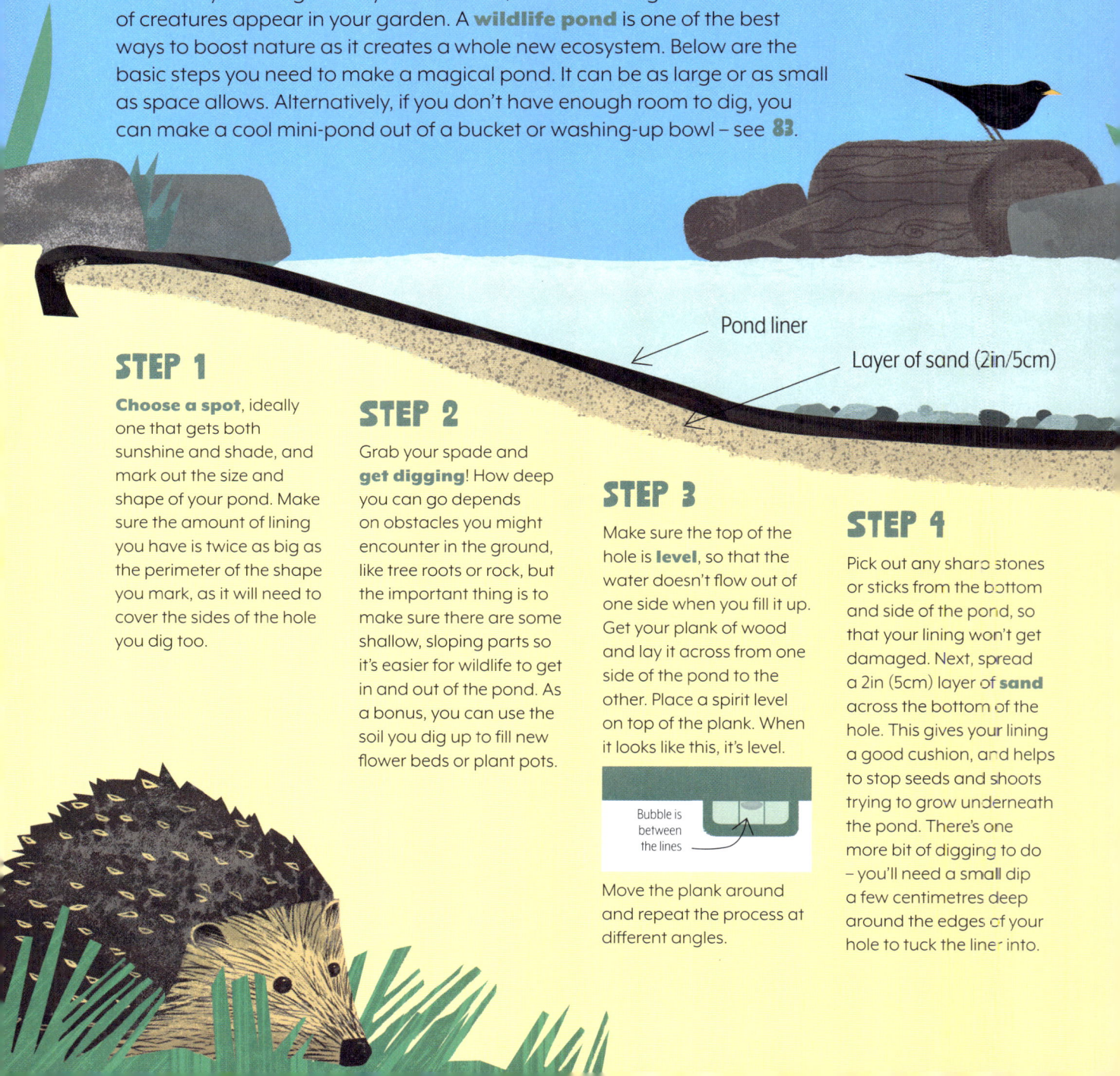

YOU WILL NEED

Flexible pond liner

Spirit level

Plank of wood

Large rocks and stones

Spade

Pond plants

Sand

Wood ramp to help animals get in and out

Fill with rainwater

STEP 5

Gently **place the liner** in the hole. Smooth it with your hand along the bottom and edges of the hole, and lay the over-hanging edges into the dip. Place rocks around the edge to secure the lining in place, and put **another** thin layer of sand on the bottom of the pond. You can also put pebbles and a few rocks on the bottom too, which make good sheltering spots for pond creatures.

STEP 6

Fill your pond with water! Using rainwater is the best option (for a great source of rainwater, see **5**), but if you only have tap water you need to leave it to stand for a few days before pouring it in. Once it's full, check the trench around the edge and use soil to fill in any new gaps caused by the liner shifting.

STEP 7

Leave the pond to settle for around a week, then put some water plants in – ideally ones that are native to your area, as this will benefit the wildlife the most. Placing **logs, rocks and plants** in the area surrounding the pond will encourage creatures to visit and hang around. It's also a good idea to use your plank of wood to create a ramp for creatures to use to get in and out of the pond.

STEP 8

The hard work is done – now you get to **enjoy watching your pond** throughout the year and seeing what wildlife it attracts to your garden. Expect everything from dragonflies to frogs and toads, bathing birds and thirsty mammals!

For an extra sprinkling of wildlife magic in your garden, see **6, 78** & **89**.

9
BUILD A RECYCLE ROBOT

Create a cool superhero robot using only recyclable material – and then when you're done, separate it out and recycle it!

If you find that too many of the items in your house are not recyclable, then you *definitely* need to try **11**.

STEP 1

Collect and sort all the rubbish from your home over a week, saving everything that has a recycle symbol on it.

STEP 2

Build your robot buddy. Let your imagination go wild – give your robot a name, a back-story, special powers and a planet-saving mission. Take or draw a picture of it and stick it next to your rubbish bin to remind everyone to *always* recycle.

STEP 3

Then... dismantle your robot and send it to be recycled! You might be a bit sad to say goodbye, but it's what your robot would have wanted – and it will all get turned into something new. Maybe even another robot...

I'll be back!

FAIRTRADE

Indicates that food growers are paid a fair price for the goods they produce.

RAINFOREST ALLIANCE

Shows food growers that work sustainably.

MADE IN... GROWN IN...

Tells you where the item was made or grown. The closer that is to where you live, the smaller its environmental footprint.

MARINE STEWARDSHIP COUNCIL

Shows that fish and other seafood products have been caught or farmed sustainably.

Locally grown

10
LEARN ABOUT LABELS

There are so many things for sale, it can be hard to figure out which products are eco-friendly, and which to avoid buying. Handily, there are some logos and labels which, if you see them on an item, tell you a little bit more about how that thing was made, and help you make a greener choice. Check out these organizations' logos and look out for them when you're on your shopping spying mission. There are lots of other local and international sustainability labels that you'll see too -- make a note of any that you spot, and look up what they mean.

11
BECOME A SHOPPING SPY

Take on a supermarket spying mission on your family's next big shop. Your challenge? Make your shopping trolley a sustainability safety zone. If an item's packaging doesn't have the recyclable symbol on it, then it doesn't go in! And if something has wrapping that really doesn't need wrapping, such as fruit and veg, out it goes! Basically, if it can't become part of a recycle robot, then it's not coming home.

What we buy makes a big difference. See **19**, **67**, **68** & **69** for planet-friendly shopping ideas.

THINK LIKE A PANDA

12
BRUSH WITH BAMBOO

If there's one thing pandas love more than anything, it's bamboo. And that's pretty smart of them, because bamboo is considered to be a **super-plant** due to its **super-quick** growing, and its **super-useful** ability to take lots of carbon out of the atmosphere, just like trees.

Now humans are starting to love bamboo too. Its hard stems are being used more and more to replace plastic in the products we use. And the cool thing is, once you cut a stem from a bamboo plant, another one is quick to grow in its place – sometimes up to an amazing 3ft (1 metre) a day!

Everything from cutlery and clothes to bedsheets and backpacks can be made from bamboo, but the simplest way to **think like a panda** is to clean your teeth with a bamboo toothbrush instead of a plastic one. The great thing about a bamboo toothbrush is that it can be composted or put in with the garden recycling after use – just remember to remove the bristles first.

PLASTIC PROBLEM

23 *BILLION* plastic toothbrushes are thrown away each year, with huge amounts ending up in the oceans. Brush with bamboo instead!

13
TURN OFF THE TAPS

It's easy to forget to turn the tap off while you're brushing your teeth. It might not seem like a lot of water going down the plughole, but do you know how much?

EXPERIMENT TIME!

Run a tap into a 2-pint (1-litre) bottle or a measuring jug (you'll need more than one) for two minutes and see how much water you collect. Don't tip it away – pour it into a bucket and use it to give your pet dragon a drink (see **57**).

Write down the number of litres you collected, double it to include your morning and evening brushes, and then multiply THAT by 365. That's how much water you could save in a year by leaving the tap off while you brush. And just imagine if everyone in the world did that too (multiply your answer by several billion)!

It's a simple but really important way of saving one of the planet's most precious resources. Using less water at home means more of it stays in important ecosystems such as rivers and lakes. If you already leave the tap off, try to persuade a friend or relative to do the same.

Can you work out approximately how many **teeth-cleans-with-taps-on** there are in...

...a swimming pool?
(178,000 gallons/675,000 litres)

...a bath tub?
(47 gallons/180 litres)

...an iceberg?
(20 billion gallons/75 billion litres)

If one teeth clean with taps on = approx. 2½ gallons (12 litres), then: bathtub (47 gallons/180 litres) = 15 teeth cleans; swimming pool (178,000 gallons/675,000 litres) = 56,000 teeth cleans; iceberg (20 billion gallons/75 billion litres) = 6 billion teeth cleans.

See **5** & **29** for more water-saving ideas.

14 GROW YOUR OWN VEG

Growing your own veg takes a bit of planning, time and patience, but tucking into a fresh and tasty plateful of something you've worked hard to produce is possibly the most enjoyable eating experience you can have. (And sharing it with someone else is even more rewarding!) If your garden is big enough you can turn a bit of lawn into a veg patch, but if space is tight, a veg planter or even a window box (see 80) are great options. You could also ask if you could help set up a school allotment, where people can all grow veg together.

Depending on what you're growing, you'll need to **sow your seeds** at the right time of year ready for harvesting several months later. Start by focusing on one crop. Carrots, beans, potatoes and beetroot are good first-time options to try in a veg patch, while plants like peas, tomatoes, peppers and chillis* are something you can try in smaller planters or patio pots. If your first harvest goes well, invite your friends to join you in creating a veg-growing club. You could grow one different type of vegetable each, and share the spoils at harvest time.

15 GROW YOUR OWN FRUIT

Growing fruit can be a much longer project than veg – it might take a good few years for an apple tree to turn from seed to first crunchy bite. But don't let that stop you: **plant a fruit tree** if you can, but get some other **smaller growing projects** going while you wait. Berry bushes and brambles, such as raspberries, blueberries and blackberries, will usually produce fruit within a season of being planted outdoors. You can also grow almost any variety of fruit in pots on your patio or even indoors – including miniature versions of full-sized fruit trees and bushes. Strawberries are great for growing in pots, and if you have a warm sunlit room or conservatory you could even try an indoor citrus tree to produce your own oranges and lemons.

As well as growing your own fruit, you can also try **'picking your own' fruit**. Having a day out at a local 'pick your own' farm is a fun way of shopping locally and seasonally, and ensuring your food is as fresh and tasty as it gets.

GROW

* Tomatoes, peppers and chillis are actually classed as fruits – even though you have them on pizza!

16 GROW YOUR OWN HERBS

Mint

Basil

Herbs are brilliant for turning a dull meal into something much more tasty – a pinch of parsley here, a sprinkle of sage there, or a touch of thyme on top adds a flavoursome zing to any cooking. A good range of herbs is essential in any serious chef's kitchen – and handily you can also **grow your own in your kitchen** too. All you need are some small pots and your choice of seeds, and a windowsill that gets the sun. It won't take too long for the first shoots to appear, then after a few weeks you should be able to start picking and using those lovely leaves. And if you start a new pot growing every couple of weeks you'll soon end up with a regular herb supply to add to your Big Cook Recipe Book (see **46**).

Low-fuss herbs
Mint, coriander and basil are easy herbs to grow on your windowsill.

Coriander

17 A SMOOTHIE A DAY

Opting for a daily home-made smoothie instead of a fizzy drink is far better for keeping both you *and* the planet healthy. You can use some of your home-grown or locally picked produce to make your own delicious **Superhero Smoothies**. All you need to do is put chopped-up fruit (or even the odd bit of veg, such as carrots and ginger) and a bit of fruit juice into a blender, give it a whizz for a minute or so, then pour and enjoy.

Experiment with different combinations, and make a note of your favourites for a Superhero Smoothie chapter of your Big Cook Recipe Book (see **46**). You could even come up with a name for your own smoothie brand, and sell it at the school summer fair to raise money for your green projects.

YOUR OWN...

Plant, nurture, harvest, prepare, enjoy... There's no better way to cut down your food miles than growing your own ingredients.

You've grown your own, now cook your own: see **43–46**.

18
SEW COOL

Sewing is a craft enjoyed by many cool people including George Clooney, Gwen Stefani, and even Thor actor Chris Hemsworth. As well as being a relaxing pastime, it's a brilliant skill to learn to help you mend clothes, and make brand new ones. All you need to get started is a needle and thread, and some material to practise on.

There are some useful simple stitching techniques to try, including the **running stitch**, **back stitch** and **cross stitch**. Once you've mastered the basics, make your first challenge **sewing a patch on to a jumper or bag**. You can buy some great patches from nature charities and wildlife companies, and you could even aim to collect patches from the different wild places you visit and sew them on to your backpack. Then, of course, the next time you get a hole in a pair of trousers or a sock, you'll be able to mend them rather than throw them away – another great service to add to your Fix & Mix Repair Shop (see **36**). Who knows, this might be your first step to becoming a super slow fashion designer!

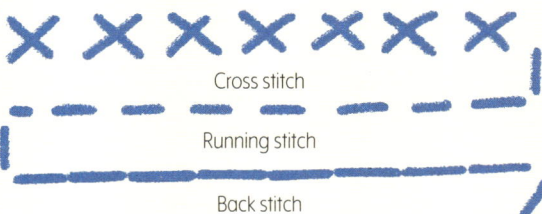

Cross stitch

Running stitch

Back stitch

19
SLOW FASHION

THINK LIKE A SLOTH

Sloths are well known for taking things *slooow* in an attempt to save energy – and you can think like a sloth by switching from fast fashion to slow fashion.

Fast fashion refers to the clothes produced and sold by big, mass-market retailers – items that are made cheaply in bulk, and sold for a low price tag but a heavy carbon cost. As well as the estimated 10 per cent of annual global carbon emissions it produces, the fashion industry also uses vast amounts of water. Making one cotton T-shirt can use more than 660 gallons (2,500 litres) of water – around the same amount that an average person drinks in three years!

Here are some things you can do to have a wardrobe a sloth would be proud of:

LOOK FOR SUSTAINABLY RESPONSIBLE BRANDS

Check the item's label to see where it was made, and from what (see **10**).

DON'T THROW CLOTHES AWAY

Mend, donate or sell them, or use the material to make something else (see **18**).

SHOP SECOND-HAND OR VINTAGE*

You can get some great gear at bargain prices this way.

MAKE NEW CLOTHES YOURSELF

You could start by getting a responsibly sourced blank T-shirt and design your own cool bit of fashion, maybe even featuring your Green Gang logo (see **17**).

* Stylish fashion from decades gone by.

Depending on the time of year and where in the world you live, you probably often have the heating on to warm your house up, or the air conditioning on to keep it cool.

Either way, this is an easy energy-saving challenge everyone can do. Start by turning your **heating down** by at least one degree, or your **air conditioning up** one degree. Your new household temperature might seem a little uncomfortable at first, but you'll quickly adapt – especially if you remember this phrase: heat the human, not the home.

Wearing more layers of clothing will soon heat you up, as will using blankets and hot water bottles. And, in reverse, layering down, opening windows and putting your feet in a bowl of cold water can help you cool down too.

20
ONE
DEGREE

21
DAFT
DRAUGHT
EXCLUDERS

Draught excluders are a great way to insulate your home. They help to save energy and keep your house warm by cutting out all those cold breezes that creep in under doors and around windows. But you don't want your draught excluders to be *boring*, so why not use your new Sew Cool skills (see **18**) to make some **funky wild worm and snake characters** that can brighten up your hall at the same time as keeping the cold air out?

MAKE IT DAFT!

Cut a piece of fabric slightly longer than the door, and about 16in (40cm) wide. Fold it in half lengthways, with the outside facing in.

Pin then sew the length and one end to make an open tube. Turn it inside out (or outside in). Then get stuffing – old (clean) socks, cut-up T-shirts and tea towels are all ideal.

Sew up the open end and decorate daftly!

GREEN STORIES

Creating, discovering and sharing stories about nature can help us all to think about the world in a new way, notice more things, and care more deeply.

22
MAKE A NATURE DOCUMENTARY

Watching a nature documentary is a great way of discovering wonderful wildlife stories from around the world. You can spend time with everything from funny-looking fish that live at the bottom of the ocean to snow-loving creatures in the Arctic, and bountiful bugs that buzz around rainforests.

Next time you're stuck indoors, instead of watching the latest movie **check out a nature series** and see if you can learn something new.

Then try **making your own nature documentary**. Pick an animal, wildlife area or green issue that interests you – it could be something that visits your garden, nature from the countryside near where you live or an unusual animal you spot when you're on holiday. Use a phone to record a short film or podcast about your topic. You'll have to be prepared and patient while filming – nature camera operators can spend weeks trying to get the right shot. Remember to include some cool facts, any problems facing the star of your programme and a 'call-to-action' (what people can do to help). When you've finished, ask your teacher or parents if they can help you share it.

CONGRATULATIONS – YOU'RE NOW A WILDLIFE DOCUMENTARY MAKER!

See **7** and **56** for location and filming tips.

23
FIND YOUR FAMILY TREE

Trees can live for a loooong time. The oldest tree in the world is thought to have been around for nearly 5,000 years, which means it was growing when the Egyptians built the pyramids. It's a Great Basin bristlecone pine, nicknamed Methuselah, in the White Mountains part of Inyo National Forest, in California, USA. There are other amazing, ancient trees in California too – towering forests of giant sequoias and giant redwoods, which can live for between 2,000 and 3,000 years.

Measuring a tree's circumference (its girth) can help you make a good guess about its age. It varies from species to species, but on average trees get around 1in (2.5cm) thicker every year, so for a 50-year-old tree a tape measure would show around 50in (125cm) when wrapped around the tree trunk.

Find a tree that might have been around for longer than the oldest person in your family. Give it a name and adopt it as **your family tree**. Think of the tales it could tell. Who planted it? What's happened in the world while it's been there? What creatures have lived in its branches? Who might have climbed it? Then draw a picture of it, alongside a list of everyone who's lived in your family while it's been alive.

OLD TREE, NEW TREE CHALLENGE

Plant a new family tree, and imagine all the stories that could happen as it grows. You can even record its journey for future generations, taking a photo of you and your family next to it on the same day each year.

The oldest tree in the world is nearly 5,000 years old, and the youngest is the seed you plant right now!

CALIFORNIA CONDOR

LIVES: USA
HABITAT: Scrub
NUMBERS: Around 350
SUPERPOWER: Long-distance gliding
CODENAME: Soar (a magnificent flyer)

NORTH AMERICA

GIANT GROUND PANGOLIN

LIVES: Central & West Africa
HABITAT: Humid forests and savannah
NUMBERS: Unknown
SUPERPOWER: Super sense of smell
CODENAME: Snuffle (a nose that can track down anythir

PYGMY THREE-TOED SLOTH

LIVES: Escudo de Veraguas Island, Panama
HABITAT: Mangroves & forests
NUMBERS: Less than 100
SUPERPOWER: Stealth
CODENAME: SlowMo (sloths are slooow)

SOUTH AMERICA

24
ASSEMBLE A SUPERHERO SQUAD

GOLDEN LION TAMARIN

LIVES: Amazon, Brazil
HABITAT: Coastal forests
NUMBERS: Around 2,500
SUPERPOWER: Disguise (looks like a lion!)
CODENAME: Mane (on account of its lion looks)

EUROPE

ASIA

AFRICA

SNOW LEOPARD

LIVES: Himalayas
HABITAT: High mountains
NUMBERS: 4,000–6,500
SUPERPOWER: Invisibility/disappearing
CODENAME: Ghost
(its nickname is
'Ghost of the Mountain')

MEDITERRANEAN MONK SEAL

LIVES: Mediterranean Sea
HABITAT: Coast and sea
NUMBERS: Fewer than 700
SUPERPOWER: Diving/underwater espionage
CODENAME: Baptiste
(means 'to dip' in French and Greek)

SUMATRAN RHINO

LIVES: Indonesia
HABITAT: Tropical forests
and lowland
swamps
NUMBERS: Less than 50
SUPERPOWER: Super strength
CODENAME: Bia
(the Greek goddess of strength)

AUSTRALIA & OCEANIA

ARCHEY'S FROG

LIVES: New Zealand
HABITAT: Damp forests
NUMBERS: 5,000–20,000
SUPERPOWER: Leaping
CODENAME: Pepe
(short for pepeketua, the Maori word for frog)

Create an awesome **team of superheroes** made up of one endangered animal from each continent. Do some endangered animal research, or use some of the ideas on this page to get started. Give each character a cool name, a personality, a catchphrase and something that every superhero needs – a special power. Then come up with a story about a cause, mission or villain that they're teaming up for or against. They could become mascots for your school or Green Gang – see **47** – or you could even produce a comic to sell and adopt an animal with the proceeds (see **55**).

25 TRAVEL BACK IN TIME

27in (70cm)

Time portal
(300 million years ago)

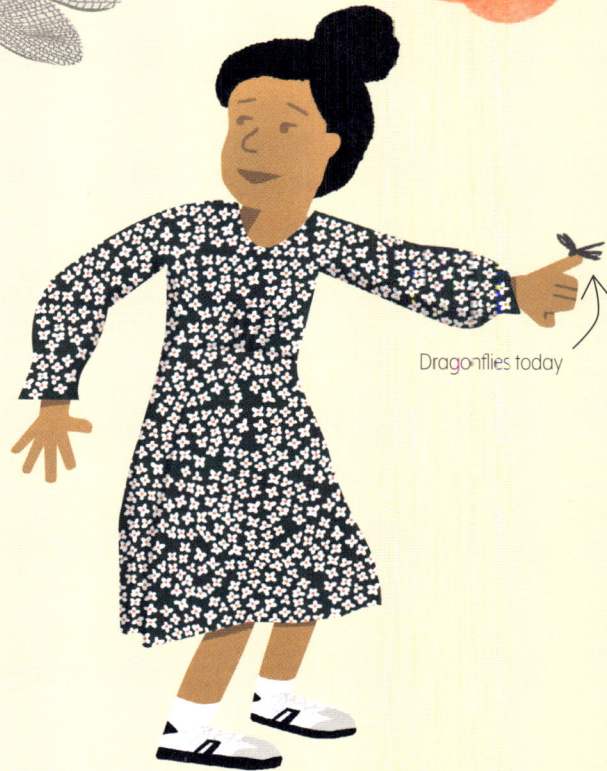

Dragonflies today

How can I time travel, you might well ask. Discover a portal? Use a magic Time Turner? Drive a DeLorean with a flux capacitor at 88mph? Well, maybe. But they're all a bit tricky, and there's a much simpler way to see what life was like in years gone by...

Dragonflies have existed on the planet for **300 million years**. They're one of the oldest surviving winged insect species, and were zipping around long before the first dinosaur plodded into being. Just think of the family stories a dragonfly could tell!

They're amazing creatures. They can spend years living underwater in ponds, lakes or rivers as nymphs, before emerging in their glorious colourful winged splendour to take to the skies. Fossils of early dragonflies show that they used to be up to five times bigger than their modern descendants, with a wingspan of 27in (70cm). They have evolved to become one of nature's most successful hunters too, with their huge eyes and fantastic flying skills giving them an almost 100 per cent success rate in hunting flies and mosquitoes (compare that to lions, who only manage to catch their prey 20 per cent of the time).

Once you've glimpsed a slice of the past, try **looking into the future**. Pick an animal that exists today and imagine how it might evolve over the next 300 million years in order to survive and thrive.

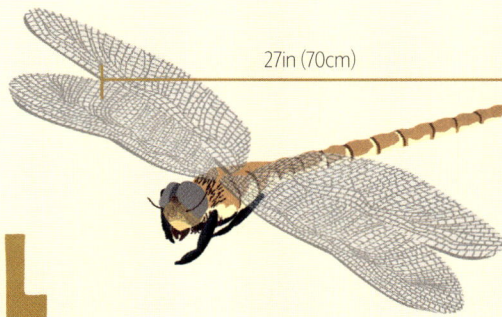

MORE ANCIENT ANIMALS

Ants
120 million years

Jellyfish
505 million years

Crabs
250 million years

Worms are another ancient animal – they've been around for 200 million years. See **32** to find out more.

Cave bear

Steller's sea cow

EXTINCT ANIMALS

What can you find out about these extinct animals?

Dodo

Passenger pigeon

Eurasian auroch

Scientists are working on a project to reintroduce a long-extinct animal to the wild – the woolly mammoth, which last wandered the Earth more than 4,000 years ago. They think that having herds of them roaming the Siberian tundra will help to restore the vast region's natural ecosystem, keeping it covered in snow and stopping carbon being released from the frozen ground.

What **animal from the past** would you like to bring back? Find as much out about it as you can, then make a poster or podcast to tell its story and campaign for reintroducing it. Think about why it became extinct, where in the world would be good for it to live now, what habitat it would need to survive, what other animals it would interact with and how it might help the environment today. Your idea could happen!

26 BRING AN ANIMAL BACK TO LIFE

27 LIGHTBULB MOMENT

In comics, lightbulbs are a symbol of having a good idea. And here's a big lightbulb moment – get rid of your lightbulbs! At least, ask your parents to get rid of your old-fashioned halogen lightbulbs, and replace them with low-energy LED lights. LED lights can give the same brightness as traditional bulbs using up to 90 per cent less energy, and they also last a lot longer too.

There's one more lightbulb idea too – get into the habit of turning off the lights whenever you leave a room (as long as there's no one left in there)!

LEDs use much less energy and last up to 25 times longer than traditional bulbs.

Go on a standby sortie. Make a list of every electronic device and appliance in your home that has a standby mode – usually ones that have a small red light. Compile an on-off checklist – a kind of school register for electrical appliances – and make sure that whoever goes to bed last in your house turns everything off before they turn in.

28 SWITCH ON TO SWITCHING OFF

TV... **OFF**
CONSOLE... **OFF**
COMPUTERS... **OFF**
CHARGERS... **OFF**
WIFI... **OFF**
SMART SPEAKERS... **OFF**
HEATING... **OFF**
(or on timer, at least)

and finally, LIGHTS... **OFF**

It's not strictly true that elephants don't wash – they actually love to play in water – but they do like to get mucky by rolling around in the mud if there's no clean water available.

You could **think like an elephant** by staying (a bit) more mucky, and saving both water and energy. One less bath a week, a shower every other day instead of every day, and wearing your clothes more than once (within reason) before putting them in the wash will all make a difference over the course of a year.

And if anyone complains, you can tell them you've adopted this motto: **I'm being less clean to be more green** (the dirtier the better)!

THINK LIKE AN ELEPHANT

29 STAY MUCKY

Most households have at least one drawer full of old chargers, phones and other electrical devices. Often they just sit there for years, 'just in case' – but most of them could easily be recycled or re-used. Have an **electrical appliance round-up** in your house. Fill as many boxes as you can with old, unused devices, and take them to a recycle point or charity (check the boxes with an adult first, just to make sure you're not accidentally giving away their prized laptop!). Go one step further by asking your school to host a community-wide electrical amnesty, where everyone can recycle their electrical clutter. Think of all the resources that would save – not to mention all the delightful empty drawer space everybody would suddenly find themselves with.

30 ELECTRICAL AMNESTY

See **35** for another use for your electrical appliances!

31
TURN LEAVES INTO COMPOST

The life of an earthworm might seem strange, wiggling around underground most of the day and night. In fact, they're fascinating creatures that play a vital role in supporting growing plants by keeping the soil fertile. One of the things worms *love* to do is feed on fallen leaves, pulling them down into their tunnels, eating them and returning the organic nutrients to the soil.

You can **think like a worm** by gathering leaves that have fallen on to concrete surfaces, such as pavements and driveways, and turning them into compost for all your springtime gardening projects.

The easiest method is to put the **leaves into a bin liner** with a few holes poked into it for drainage, tie it up and leave it outside to stew. Alternatively, you can **make a simple leaf compost box** in your garden using chicken wire and bamboo canes.

WORM WAITING WARNING

It can take up to TWO WHOLE YEARS for the leaves to break down, so read on to discover another way to be wowed by worms while you wait...

See **91** for another compost idea.

YOU WILL NEED

A large glass jar or fishbowl.

Add a cloth lid to stop your worms escaping! Use elastic bands to hold it on. Don't forget to pop a few small air holes in the cloth.

Leave a gap of a few centimetres above the top layer.

Place a few leaves on the top layer for your worms to feed on.

The most important thing? Add worms, of course!

Alternate layers of sand and moist soil, starting with sand at the bottom.

32
MAKE A WORMERY

Ever wanted a **worm's-eye view of the world**? A wormery is a neat way to get to know what these wonderful wigglers get up to underground. Follow the steps above, then put your wormery in a cool, dark place. Check in on your subterranean pals regularly, making sure the soil doesn't dry out. You could even name them (Wayne, Wanda, Wormeo and Juliet. Get creative with your 'W' names!). Just remember to put your new friends back in the garden after a couple of weeks so that they can carry on the good work.

33
RACE A SUNFLOWER

Getting into growing things is a great green skill to develop, and sunflowers are one of the easiest and most satisfying plants to start out with as they can become very tall, very quickly. To make this activity even more entertaining, here's a fun challenge. On the day you plant a sunflower seed, **mark your height on a chart**. Once a week, measure your sunflower and record how tall it is – and update your height too. See how much you can grow before the sunflower gets as tall as you!

SUPER SUNFLOWERS

Sunflowers are more than just nice, cheerful flowers that brighten up a garden – they have **big benefits for wildlife** too. The head of a large sunflower can contain thousands of tiny florets (little flowers), which bees and birds love to feed on, and which eventually turn into seeds. Sunflowers are also great for making the soil nice and healthy as its roots suck up and remove bad things such as chemicals and metals from the ground, which helps other plants growing nearby.

34
HARVEST A SUNFLOWER

With just a little help, sunflowers can continue to be great providers even after they've finished growing. Once your sunflower has faded, you can turn it into a natural bird feeder by snipping the stem near the head, tying some string around it, and hanging it from a tree branch or post. Or, **follow the steps below and collect hundreds of seeds** from the flower head to use as bird food over the winter, to plant to grow new flowers or add to your Super Seed Superstore (see **38**), or even as an ingredient in your Big Cook Recipe Book (see **46**).

STEP 1
When your flower starts to turn brown and dry out, **cover the head** with a paper bag to protect the seeds.

STEP 2
Once all the petals have fallen off, snip off the head, and **brush it** with your hand so the seeds fall off (put a tray underneath to catch them).

STEP 3
Spread the seeds out to dry indoors, then **store them in a container** over winter in a dark, cool place. These are good for planting or your Super Seed Superstore (see **38**).

STEP 4
If you want to use the seeds as food, either for birds or yourself, crunch the collected seeds with a rolling pin to **crack the outer shells**.

CRUNCH!
CRUNCH!

STEP 5
Tip your cracked seeds into a bowl of water. The outside bits should float, and the **seeds will sink to the bottom** – these are the edible parts!

Husks
Seeds will sink!

STEP 6
Scoop out the husks, then pour the water with the **inner seeds** through a sieve. Once dry, store them in a container, ready to use in a recipe, or eat as a snack.

SWAP & SHARE

Sharing is caring, so the saying goes, and sharing skills, ideas, things and seeds will definitely help make your world greener.

35 LIBRARY OF THINGS

One study in the USA estimates that the average household has a staggering 300,000 items in it! And if there are that many things in one house, just imagine how much stuff there is in a *whole street*...

Much like in a library where one book can be enjoyed by many people, a community 'library of things' means your whole neighbourhood can pool their resources, consume and spend less, and connect more. The library can be a list of who has what, rather than a physical store. You just need to **sign up a few friends and neighbours** and get the swapping action going – anything from ladders to hedge trimmers, screwdrivers to bicycles. The more we share our resources, the kinder we are to the planet.

36
FIX & MIX

As well as sharing *things*, sharing *skills* can be a great way for everyone to use less stuff. Tips and rubbish sites are full of broken or old items that have been thrown away, to be replaced by a new model. But within your community there will be people with all kinds of different skills, with the ability to repair and fix all kinds of different things.

Get started by taking this **double fixing challenge**. If people don't want the fixed items for themselves any more, they could be given away, added to your Library of Things or donated to a charity.

A DOUBLE FIXING CHALLENGE

PART 1
Learn to fix something that's broken. Start off with a simple task, and ask for guidance from an adult. Every time you learn a new technique, you'll become more confident at repairing things.

PART 2
Ask a teacher or family member to help you recruit a team of volunteers and **set up a pop-up repair shop** at your school or community centre. It could be a one-off, or a monthly event, where people with broken items – furniture, electronics, bikes – can bring them for your crew of volunteers to have a go at fixing.

37
SPREAD THE MAGIC

Imagine if you could hold in your hands one of the **most powerful, magical objects in the world**. An item with the ability to transport you instantly to anywhere on the planet, and change it for the better. Well, here's the exciting thing – you already are...

... **a BOOK**!

Think of the books you own like boxes of tricks – they need to be opened to come to life. So read as many inspirational nature books as you can, but don't put them back on your shelf when you've finished. Instead, **start a nature book library or swap shop** with your friends. It could begin with a simple box outside your house for people on your street to put in, and take out, nature books – but who knows how big it could become? The *more* people that get involved, the more the library will grow, and the *more* the magic will spread as *more* people start to learn about and love nature.

38
SUPER SEED SUPERSTORE

From maple and sycamore whirlers that fly like helicopters and dandelion parachutes that blow on the breeze, to sticky burdock grains that hitch a furry ride and fruit pips that get pooped, seeds are *very* clever at getting where they need to go. There's another way seeds can get a helping hand to go and grow – Green Superheroes like you!

Follow the steps to the right to collect as many seeds as you can to **create a super seed superstore**. Label the jars, and when planting time comes around share them with your friends, neighbours, classmates and teachers. If you encourage them to save and store too, you'll end up with a mega seed bank that will help all kinds of plants spread and flourish across your neighbourhood.

STEP 1 | PICK

Let seeds fully develop on the plant before you pick them. Different seeds are ready at different times.

STEP 2 | STORE

Most seeds can be kept in air-tight containers, or envelopes, although some need to be stored in water – check which is right for your plant.

STEP 3 | SHARE & SOW

Plant some of the seeds yourself, but give the rest out or add them to your super seed superstore. The wider the seeds are shared, the wilder your neighbourhood becomes.

A-G

H-R

S-Z

SEEDS TODAY

Use your seeds for Sprinkle Sorties too – see **90**.

39
S.O.S. (SELL OLD STUFF)

Stuff. We all have it. Usually an *awful lot* of it – all those things we've bought, collected or been given over the years. And normally, the inevitable end for all that **stuff** is to be kept for years but never used, then thrown away. But one person's clutter can be another's treasure.

Sort through all your **stuff**, and identify anything you haven't used recently, or don't *really* need any more. Get the rest of your family to do the same, then hold a big garage sale, or take a slot at a car boot sale.

Every item you sell means you're contributing to the *circular economy* (see **64**) – someone is making use of your old things, rather than buying something that's brand new, meaning less **stuff** going into landfill, and less new **stuff** being made.

Put the proceeds towards a green cause – either something you need to carry out one of the activities in this book, or donate it to a nature project or charity.

40
GIVE UP SOMETHING

This might be the simplest challenge in this book, but also the hardest: **give up one thing that you love**. It could be sweets, toys, trading cards or video games – anything that you normally spend money on – and put it towards something that's good for nature.

You don't have to give it up for ever, but try setting a fundraising target that you're working towards. It could be the cost of a new tree to plant (see **23**), the price of a water butt for your garden (see **5**) or even a wildlife camera (see **56**) – and don't give up on giving up until you hit the total.

You'll feel a great sense of achievement when you get there, and you'll show to everybody that you're really committed to becoming a Green Superhero. You might even inspire others to do the same.

41 BIRTHDAY BONUS

You can take the 'Give up something' challenge one step further by striking a **birthday bargain** with your parents. Rather than requesting a bunch of big presents for your next celebration, ask instead for them to donate to a good nature cause: adopting an animal (see **55**), joining a nature charity or your Big Wild Project (see **94**). But the bargain is that *they* have to do the same on *their* next celebration too!

42 SWAP SCREEN FOR GREEN

TVs; phones; tablets; games consoles; computers; VR headsets.... There's no doubt that screen-time and entertainment time go hand in hand. But the longer we spend glued to our screens, the less time we have for nature*, and for each other. Try **making one day a week entirely screen-free** – not just for you, but for your whole household. If *you're* doing it, *they're* doing it too! If you *really* can't manage a day, try starting with an afternoon, evening or even just an hour – just as long as nobody looks at a screen at all during that time.

The other part of the challenge? While the screens are off, everyone must do something together in nature. It doesn't matter if that's going on a hike (see **52**), gardening, bird watching, or even having a SpoGomi competition (see **61**), just as long as you're enjoying the outdoors, and each other's company.

If the weather is *really* bad on your screen-free day, you can all settle down with a good book from your nature library (see **37**).

* Unless you're making a nature documentary – see **22**.

THE BIG COOK

Four ways to cut the carbon footprint of the food you eat – and enjoy terrifically tasty meals at the same time.

43 BATCH FOR THE FUTURE

Saving extra portions when cooking is a good habit to get into to reduce food waste, but **batch cooking** takes things to another level. Batch cooking is having one mega cooking session where you make enough food in one go to provide several meals to store and enjoy throughout the week, saving time, energy and resources.

It requires some careful planning and preparation, so appoint yourself as **head chef** and draw up a Sunday afternoon batch cook plan for your team of assistant chefs (your parents and siblings) to follow. You can even liven things up by making a fun **batch-cook beats** playlist of food-themed tunes and turn it into a big cook-up bash.

BATCH COOK TIPS

- Use clear containers, and label them so that you can remember what you've made
- Choose ingredients that can go in more than one dish
- Make some sauces and side dishes to mix things up throughout the week
- Experiment: try at least one new dish a week, and you'll soon have a big selection to choose from
- Store in small portions, in case people want to eat different things, or someone misses a meal

44 TEA FOR TWO

Having a friend round after school for tea (or dinner, or supper – whatever you prefer to call it) is always great fun – lots of chatting, laughter, and, sometimes, even a tasty meal. There's another benefit to it too: sharing meals is planet friendly, saving on cooking effort, energy and time, and reducing food waste. Start by inviting a good friend and their family round for one evening meal. Then, see if you can make it a weekly event – sometimes at your house, sometimes at theirs. If *that* goes well, you could try inviting *other* friends and *their* families for tea (or dinner, or supper), or sharing your batch cooking (see **43**). Imagine the time and effort you could save if you got *seven* families involved, meaning each house only cooks one big batch or meal each a week and swaps and shares seven different meals – a **Super Seven Supper Club**.

45 SOUPER-HERO SOUP

Not all superheroes wear capes – but they definitely should all be powered by **delicious home-made soup**! Inventing and making tasty soups is a great thing to do with left-over ingredients, and is another way to cut down on your food waste. Once you've come up with a new soup concoction, be sure to write down the ingredients in your Big Cook Recipe Book (see **46**), and chill or freeze any spare leftovers to add to your Big Batch stockpile (see **43**). If you have a thermos flask you can even have your soup in your rebooted packed lunch (see **68**).

ALL YOU NEED TO MAKE A SOUPER-HERO SOUP

- An Assistant Chef (also known as an adult)
- A large pan with some heated butter or oil
- Some chopped veg, such as onion, celery, carrot or leek, to form a base
- A spot of seasoning (see **16**)
- Some water or 'stock' (savoury flavoured liquid)
- Any other ingredients you like – embrace your inner soup souper-hero and be bold in your experiments!

46 BIG COOK RECIPE BOOK

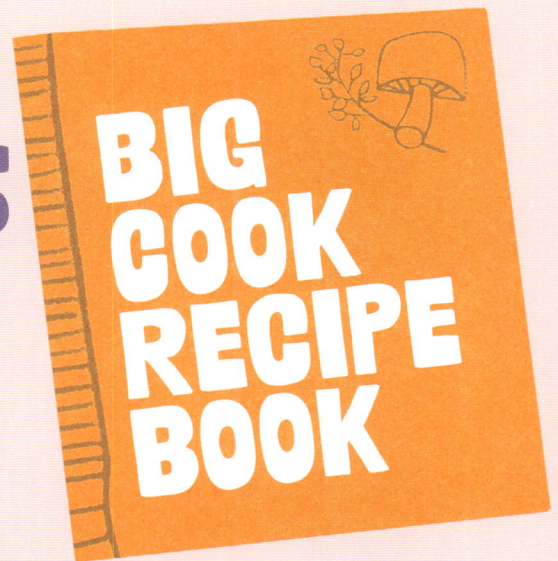

We all have our favourite things to eat – sweet strawberries, juicy grapes, tangy blueberries, bitter Brussels sprouts (OK, maybe not the Brussels sprouts). And it's definitely tempting to want to buy these things all year round. But most fruit and vegetables have a limited time of the year when they're grown and harvested in the country where you live.

The rest of the time they're likely to be flown in from other countries, or have used a lot of energy and packaging to be produced out of season or preserved. Eating seasonal fruit and veg is a really good way to reduce your food footprint. It also means the things you eat will always be fresher and tastier, and you'll start to look forward to your changing menu at different times of the year.

As you take on the Big Cook challenges, compile all your new and favourite recipes into your very own seasonal **Green Superhero Recipe Book**, and divide it into 12 chapters – one for each month of the year, based on seasonal ingredients. When it's complete, you could even give copies of it to your friends, family and Super Seven Supper Club buddies (see **44**). And don't forget to add your special celebrity chef signature!

47 GREEN GANG

You're well on your way to Green Superhero status (almost half-way!), but you'll be even stronger as part of a **Super Green Gang**. Gather together a group of nature-loving friends, and come up with some planet-positive plans – as well as a **cool Green Gang name**. It could be just a small set of pals who enjoy doing outdoor things together, or you could try making it an official school club with regular members' meet-ups. Either way, a Super Green Gang is a great way to collaborate on ideas, get nature projects going (see **94**) and tackle important issues.

48 BEE POSITIVE

The news is often filled with negative stories about the planet, which can be worrying. But good news happens all the time too! Make a **Bee Positive Good News Diary**, and fill it with one positive story about nature every week. It could be something about the success of a local wildlife project, an increase in numbers of a threatened species in a different country or a new sustainable invention or idea that you've read about.

Don't forget to add all the positive things that you've done for the planet to the diary too. You could even start a **Bee Positive notice board or newsletter** at school for everybody to add their good nature news to.

49 GREEN HAIR

Sometimes you need to do something **striking** to get attention. Ask your school's permission to organize a **Green Hair Week** (or at least a *Green Highlights Week*) as part of a 100 Ways To Save The Planet fundraising and awareness campaign. Even better if you can get your teachers or parents to go green haired too! You and your **Green Gang** could pick a nature theme or wildlife project (see **94**) that you want to showcase and support, and share some of the activities from this book too.

Pencil & paper

Your imagination

WHAT COULD YOU POWER BY PEDAL?

50 PEDAL AN INVENTION

Inventions usually come about as an attempt to solve a problem. Your challenge? Use your imagination to design a **pedal-powered invention** that tackles an environmental issue. It could be an idea that saves energy, cuts down on pollution or does something positive for nature. Remember, no idea is too silly or too complicated – *everything* we use today began as a little spark in *someone's* imagination.

Get started with just a pencil and paper and sketch out your idea. If nothing comes to mind, don't worry – try doodling and see what appears. Keep refining your idea until you're happy with it. Then you could always send it off to a big company, or even your country's leader (see **100**), and see if someone can turn your idea into reality. Who knows? You might have come up with something that makes a big difference.

51 GREEN LAWS

Imagine if you were in charge of... well... everything! Think of **five green laws** that you would introduce to help nature. You can make them as realistic or as revolutionary as you want – and about anything you want, from transport, energy and food, to trees, recycling or animals – as long as your laws are designed to change things for the better. Write them up as your **Green Manifesto**, and share with your Green Gang too. You could even send them to someone who really is in charge of everything and see if they like your ideas (see **100**).

52

EXPAND YOUR WILD HORIZONS

Taking a walk in nature is one of the best things you can do to feel healthy and happy, so having a go-to set of your favourite outdoor places to head to for a hike is really important. But it's also great to set aside time to **discover new wild places** – after all, every place that's on your favourites list was new to you once.

Start by visiting the nearest local nature reserve that you've never been to before. It might be a protected stretch of river or coast, a bird sanctuary, a wild meadow, a wetland area or even a national park. Wherever you pick, enjoy **exploring new wild frontiers**, and finding out about the mission of the organization that runs it and how you can support them.

Then, draw up **a wild wish list of 10 other new places** you'd *love* to visit, and see if you can tick them all off over the next year. There's a very good chance that some of them will end up becoming new favourites.

Inviting a friend on a walk is a simple activity that might not seem like it's going to make much difference to the future of the planet. But there's an ancient Chinese proverb that says: *A journey of a thousand miles begins with a single step* – and a walk with a Green Superhero like you could be the first step on your friend's journey to falling in *love* with nature too.

Pick one of your favourite places – it could even be one of your new wild discoveries (see above) – and invite someone you know who doesn't normally get out into nature to go with you. You don't even have to tell them why you're taking them. The walk, your surroundings, the good company (you) and your enthusiasm for all the things you've learned about nature are all that's needed to start your friend's thousand-mile journey to becoming another Green Superhero like you.

53

TAKE A FRIEND ON A WALK

 These are all great things to do on your screen-free day – see **42**.

LOOK FOR THE PLUES

PLUES

Most creatures are pretty good at making themselves scarce when people are around, but just because you can't *see* them doesn't mean you can't figure out what might be lurking nearby. A great way to make any walk or expedition even more exciting is to turn it into **a top tracker detective mission**.

CLUES

Your assignment: find evidence of what creatures might live around the area you're visiting by seeking out **CLUES** and **PLUES**! All you need is a notepad and pen, and a good eye (and ear and nose) for detail!

CLUES are things like footprints, burrows or nests, squeaks and chirps that might give you useful detective hints. But **PLUES** are the most useful-yet-yucky sort of tracker evidence of all – **poo clues**! Animal droppings come in all different shapes and sizes, and, if you take a bit of time to swot up on stools, can tell you exactly what creature left it, and even how recently it was there, depending on how 'fresh' the droppings are.

Deer

Take a note, or draw a picture, of the **CLUES** and **PLUES** you find on your missions, and where you spotted the evidence. If you don't recognize what animal they belong to, try to identify them at home using a guidebook or online, and add that information to your records. After a few missions you'll soon find you've turned into a top **PLUE** tracker, able to tell your deer droppings from your fox faeces with one quick glance – a nature skill that's *definitely* not to be sniffed at! And once you know what animals might be around, you've got more chance of seeing them in the flesh in future, and helping protect their habitats.

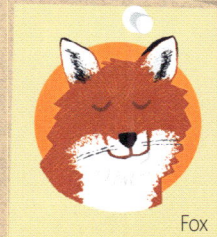
Fox

Hare

SUSPECTS ?

Plues will definitely help you on your Learn Your Mammals quest – see **93**.

47

55 ADOPT AN ANIMAL

A nice way to help an endangered species is to adopt an animal. Conservation organizations rely on donations from people who care about nature to carry out their work, and run animal adoption schemes so that you can support a particular species.

That doesn't mean if you adopt an orangutan it'll come and live in your house – as fun as that might be. But it does mean that you'll be **helping in the efforts to provide a better future** for your chosen animal, and you'll usually be sent some cool information and updates about its progress. It's a really worthwhile thing to put your pocket money towards (see **40** and **41**), and if you don't quite have enough, ask a parent if they'll match what you put in. (See **24** for more on endangered animals.)

56 NIGHTS, CAMERA, ACTION!

Setting up a wildlife camera is a brilliant way of seeing what creatures come and go on your patch. There's nothing more exciting than checking out what wild activities went on outside overnight as you munch on your morning cereal!

A good camera can be quite expensive, so it might be something that you could persuade your school to invest in and share around as part of a nature project, or for your Green Gang (see **47**) to raise funds towards.

You can also check out online wildlife cameras from further afield – all around the world, in fact. There are some fantastic wilderness webcams run by conservation organizations that live stream everything from badgers in Britain and condors in California, to warthogs, zebras and elephants at watering holes in South Africa. Tune into these every morning before school and breakfast will never be boring again!

57
BRING UP A PET DRAGON

Houseplants are a wonderful way of getting closer to nature *inside* your home. One of the easiest types to look after is the Dragon Tree (also known as *Dracaena marginata*). Keep one in your room and **adopt it as your pet** – one that you feed and water, talk to and love. Give it a cool dragony name, and take pride in watching it grow from a little flame of a baby dragon into a huge, roaring elder dragon.

Snake plant

Spider plant

Chinese evergreen

There are plenty of other plants of different shapes and sizes in garden centres that are great for growing indoors.

HAPPIER HOUSE

Just like plants that grow outside, **indoor plants help to make the air cleaner** and are good for the atmosphere – the more you have in your house, the greater the benefit. Having plants inside makes people feel happier, and gives them a stronger connection to nature. Looking after a houseplant will also help you understand more about growing plants outdoors.

58 LEARN YOUR BIRDS

Loon

Start by **learning about one new bird a day, for 10 days**. To begin with, pick birds that live close to you – either ones that are native all year round, or that migrate and are only there for a few months in the year – so that you have a good chance of seeing them. A bird identifying app, website or book will be a great help.

Things to find out about include size, colour of feathers, beak and tail shape, the differences in appearance between males, females and juveniles (young birds), what song they sing and where they nest. You can also make your own **spotter's list** containing key facts to help tick them off when you see them.

You should find that once you know 10 birds well, you'll start to notice them more when you're out and about, and it will become much easier to identify other birds too. Now you're well on your way to becoming a **bird expert**! If you already know your local birds, try learning about 10 new birds from another part of the world.

Green pheasant

59 FEED THE BIRDS

Redstart

White-tailed eagle

60 BIRD B&B

Making and installing garden, patio or balcony **bird feeders** is guaranteed to attract more birdlife to your patch. **Fat balls** provide a good source of food year-round, but especially in winter when birds need to stay insulated and keep their body weight up. They're easy (and fun) to make, and you can either hang them individually from tree branches, or load them into a wire-framed fat ball feeder.

Other hanging serving suggestions for your mixture include filling coconut shells or hollowed-out oranges, and pasting it around the edge of toilet rolls, pierced with small sticks that birds can use as a perch.

FOR A FAT BALL FEAST... YOU WILL NEED

Pine cone

Length of string

Bird seed mix

Mixing bowl

Block of lard or suet (but NOT cooking fat)

STEP 1   Warm the block of lard or suet to room temperature in a mixing bowl, so it's soft and squidgy.

STEP 2   Pour some healthy bird seed mix into the bowl and mash it all together. Get those hands STICKY!

STEP 3   To hang the balls individually, first tie some garden string around a small pine cone, then sculpt the mixture around it, leaving a good length of string hanging out. If you're putting them into a seed dispenser, sculpt into a ball shape.

STEP 4   Put them in the fridge to set. Serve alfresco, and tell the birds it's tea time!

You've laid on a feast, now you need to **provide some accommodation** to encourage your feathery friends to stick around. Different species need different sized houses, so pick one that will be good for the type of birds in your area. Organizations such as the RSPB in the UK or the US National Audubon Society are good places to buy them from. You can even purchase plain ones and decorate them yourself, or follow the DIY bird box building instructions on their websites.

You could also put up **an extra holiday home** to attract visitors – the migratory birds that visit seasonally, like swifts and swallows. Both of these species need special types of nest boxes that sit higher up on buildings, to allow them to swoop in.

Once you've installed your **Bird B&B**, the next thing to do is... wait. You might see the birds that come for the food investigating for a while: being curious, checking out the property and the neighbourhood, before they make any decisions about moving in permanently. But when they do, it's fascinating to watch them come and go as they decorate and furnish their new home, pop in and out on food gathering missions, and hopefully lay some eggs. And, all being well, you might eventually witness the magnificent, nerve-jangling moment when their **fledgling chicks take their first flight** into the big wide world from the nest that you put up, just for them.

Wren

Once you've completed these activities, don't forget to redo your garden bird count – see 4.

BE MORE...

We can all be inspired by each other when it comes to caring for nature and making the world a better place. Check out these positive practices from different parts of our planet...

BE MORE JAPANESE

JAPAN

61 DISCOVER SPOGOMI

Did you know you can become a World Champion – at *litter picking*? The Japanese sport of **SpoGomi** involves teams of three racing to collect as much rubbish as possible in one hour. They then sort the litter into different categories, such as recyclable metal cans and plastic bottles, with points awarded for the amounts collected. There's even a **SpoGomi World Cup**.

A SpoGomi contest with your friends is a fun way to clear up your neighbourhood. There are lots of benefits: animals have less chance of coming to harm from eating litter, more rubbish gets recycled, and everything looks nicer, so people are more likely to want to keep it that way. And who knows, you might even become a World Champion one day!

62
SWITCH TO RENEWABLES

Costa Rica in Central America is one of the greenest countries in the world. Not only are its tropical forests home to the greatest density of biodiversity on the planet, but it gets almost all of its electrical energy from **renewable sources**. The main supply is hydroelectricity, thanks to all the rain that falls there, and the rest comes from biomass, solar power and wind power.

You can **become more Costa Rican** by persuading your household to get as much of its energy from renewable sources as possible – whether that's switching your home energy supplier to a greener provider, installing solar panels on your roof, trading in a petrol or diesel-powered vehicle for an electric one, or ditching the car altogether and using pedal power (see **65**) to get around instead. Every switch away from polluting fossil fuels is a step in a greener direction.

COSTA RICA

BE MORE COSTA RICAN

jogga
(jog)

➕

plocka
(picking up)

🟰 plogging!

63
GO PLOGGING

It's well known that taking regular outdoor exercise helps improve your physical health and boost your spirits. The Swedish activity of **plogging** takes that a step further, doubling the feel-good factor by combining a run or jog with a clean-up mission. All you need to become a plogger is some regular running gear, a bin bag and a pair of gloves (a litter grabber is a handy optional extra). Go on a normal run, but every time you see some rubbish, pop it in your bag. Simple as that!

You might feel initially that *your* plog on its own isn't going to make much difference, but what started out as one Swedish person's effort to do something about cleaning the streets of Stockholm has already grown into **a movement of more than 3 million ploggers worldwide**, including some major organized plogging events. So who knows – by plogging the streets around where you live, you might spark a local plogging craze of your own that transforms your community.

64
GET INTO UPCYCLING

The Danish capital of Copenhagen is pretty innovative when it comes to re-using things in a green way. Much of the city's heating supply comes from turning waste into energy and even the waste power plant building has more than one use – its huge sloping roof features a ski slope, a hiking trail and a climbing wall! Danish designers think in a 'circular' way too: several new housing projects have been built in Copenhagen using **'upcycling' – turning something old into something new**. Upcycled materials used include old bricks from demolished buildings, surplus concrete from the city's metro, offcuts of wood from a flooring company and glass windows that have been left over from office refurbishments – all of which helps to cut down the construction carbon footprint.

You can be more Danish by doing your own upcycling project. It could be re-painting or re-covering some tatty furniture, converting a boring old wall or flat roof into a green space, or turning wooden pallets or fence panels into something exciting like a tree-house. You could even add your new upcycling skills to your Fix & Mix collective's services – see **36**.

65 JUMP ON YOUR BIKE

Cycling is more than a way of getting around in the Netherlands – it's a way of life. It's a perfect place for bike riders – it's very flat and it helps that there are more than 22,000 miles (35,000km) of dedicated bike paths across the country. The average Dutch adult pedals about 600 miles (1,000km) a year, and children and teenagers cycle even further.

Where you live might not be as bike-friendly as the Netherlands, but don't let that put you off. If you can **replace one motor journey a week with a bike ride** you're already bringing down your carbon footprint. If you get a friend to be your bike buddy and do the same, that's double green points. And the more people who cycle in your area, **the more Dutch it should become**. If you don't have a bike of your own, there are bike borrowing schemes in many places, or you might be able add bike sharing to your Library of Things – see 35.

66 DISCOVER FRILUFTSLIV

Norway is ranked as one of the happiest countries in the world to live in, and a large part of that is due to the philosophy of friluftsliv. **Friluftsliv translates as 'free air life'**, and involves making a commitment to spend time doing things in the outdoors, whatever the weather. The type of activity is not so important – it could be anything from climbing a mountain to paddling in a stream, or having a picnic. The crucial thing is to connect with nature and other people, be curious about your outdoor surroundings, be active, and trying and learning new things. By getting into the habit of being a little more Norwegian, even when it rains, your love of nature and own wellbeing should continue to grow.

NORWAY

SWEDEN

DENMARK

The NETHERLANDS

THINK LIKE AN ORANGUTAN

Orangutans are a brilliant example of animals that exist in harmony with their environment. They eat, drink and sleep high up in the tropical rainforests of south-east Asia, and 'orangutan' actually means 'person of the forest' in Malay. But they're also particularly at risk to habitat loss caused by deforestation to make space for palm oil plantations.

Palm oil is used in all sorts of products, from bread, biscuits and bars to cosmetics, pet supplies and fuel. It comes from the fruit of oil palm trees, which produce a much bigger harvest than other sources of vegetable oil. Because of this, avoiding products that contain palm oil isn't the best solution, because alternative vegetable oils need even more land to grow. But there are important actions you can take, including looking out for the RSPO logo. RSPO stands for the Roundtable on Sustainable Palm Oil, and is a scheme that means that the palm oil comes from a responsible producer.

67
BE A PERSON OF THE FOREST

Start **thinking like an orangutan** by doing some **palm oil private investigating**. Look through your cupboards and find five things that have palm oil in their ingredients but which *don't* have the RSPO logo, and then choose an alternative that does for your next supermarket shop. Then, send a message to the company that made those products, and to your regular supermarket, to say why you're switching to an orangutan-friendly alternative (and add a little picture of a 'person of the forest' too).

68
PACKED LUNCH REBOOT

Give your **packed lunch a planet-positive reboot** by replacing anything that's not eco-friendly with something that is to turn it into a nurdle-free, palm-oil friendly, low air-mile, batch-cooked, home-grown, locally sourced lunch fit for a superhero. Remember to think about packaging too: flasks or reusable water bottles, fabric or bamboo boxes, and even beeswax food wrap all help to lessen your lunch impact. You can apply the same logic to refreshments you buy when you're out and about too. Carry a reusable water bottle, and INSIST that any coffee drinkers in your family take their own reusable cup on their daily work journey instead of buying drinks in disposable containers.

69
SAY NO TO NURDLES

Nurdles are tiny balls of plastic, less than 3/16in (5mm) in size, that are used to make plastic products. They are so small that spilt and discarded nurdles slip through water filters, and end up in rivers, seas and on beaches, harming marine life which often ends up mistaking them for food.

Microbeads are similar to nurdles, but even smaller. They're present in products that *aren't* made out of plastic, including a large number of things you use in the bathroom, such as face wash and toothpaste, in order to give them a rougher feel.

You can help by taking the same action as with palm oil products. **Do a stock-take** of any single-use or unnecessary plastic purchases you can ditch. Then look to see which of your bathroom items contain microbeads: the Beat The Microbead campaign has an online product checker that will tell you if your shampoo is a suspect, or your toothpaste is a troublemaker. Finally, let the product makers and supermarkets know that nurdles and microbeads are no longer welcome in your house.

See **9 – 12** for more sustainable shopping suggestions.

70
BATTERY RECHARGE

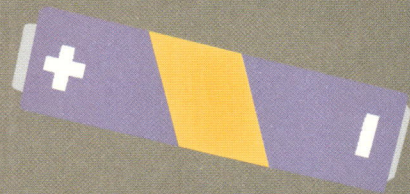

Billions of single-use batteries are produced each year, but only a small percentage are recycled. The resources and energy used to make them, and the unfriendly chemicals that can leak into the ground if not recycled, gives them a huge eco-footprint.

Give your household's battery impact this simple two-step boost:

STEP 1

Gather up all the used batteries lying around and take them to a recycle point – you can find often find them in places like supermarkets, libraries and even schools.

STEP 2

Switch to rechargeable batteries. They're a bit more expensive, and you'll need to buy a charger to get started, but you can use them hundreds of times, seriously reducing your costs *and* battery impact on the environment in the long term.

CHANGE HOW YOU TRAVEL

Penguins used to fly. But over time, they figured out that taking to the sky wasted too much energy, and they could get along perfectly fine by swimming (and waddling). Now they don't fly at all. You can think like a penguin and save energy by making changes to the way you travel

71 ON YOUR MARKS, OFFSET, GO...

One way to measure how your travelling habits affect the planet is to compare the rough amount of carbon emissions caused by *one* person travelling *one* kilometre by *different* modes of transport. Flying has the worst impact, while walking has the best...

While walking (or cycling, scooting or skating) is *definitely* the greenest way to travel, not to mention good exercise, there are times when you have to make a long plane or car journey. But you can always ask your parents to use an online calculator to work out the emissions your journey created, then contribute towards a scheme that helps to **offset** or **remove** that same amount of carbon dioxide from the atmosphere.

72 STAYCATION LOCATION

You *probably* don't book the holidays in your household, but you *can* plant this seed of an idea with your parents: make your next family **vacation** a **staycation**. Ask if you can choose a destination closer to home that you don't need to fly to. You could try an area of countryside or coast that you've always wanted to visit, or even stay at home and do day trips to places that you haven't explored before. If you don't tend to fly as a family anyway, ask if you can invite a friend who does to join you on your next staycation.

The penguin footprint carbon emissions guide:
Travel by plane has the worst impact per person, per kilometre, while walking has the most positive impact:

Flying | Petrol/diesel cars | Bus | Electric cars | Boat | Train | Walk (or cycle, scoot or skate)

73
THOUGHT OF TRAINS?

An electric-powered train journey can produce up to 10 times fewer emissions per passenger than a flight to the same destination. So here's another seed to sow: make your next longer-haul holiday a trip by train*. It might take a couple of days to get there, but the journey will become part of the adventure. By day, turn the trip into a scenic safari. Watch how the landscape changes the further you travel, and see how many different types of trees, birds and creatures you can spot. By night, cosy up in a sleeper cabin, and tell each other some Superhero Squad stories (see 24).

74
SKATES ON FOR SCHOOL

Mornings can be a rush – sleeping through a snoozing alarm, guzzling down your breakfast, and jumping in the car to get to school with seconds to spare. If that sounds familiar, try changing the story by making a new routine. Get up a bit earlier, have an energising Superhero Smoothie breakfast (see 17), and leave plenty of time to walk (or cycle, scoot or skate) to school instead of being driven.

If you *already* walk to school, see if you can encourage a friend who *doesn't* to join you. Or you could even ask your teacher about setting up a school walking bus, where children across the neighbourhood all walk in together.

75
CAR POOL POSSE

At rush hour, roads get clogged with traffic pumping out exhaust fumes, many with only one person in each vehicle. Often, all those three-quarter empty cars are going to or from the same place. Imagine if they all teamed up and shared lifts – emissions and congestion would be so much less! Think about the regular car trips that your family makes – your school journey, getting to clubs and activities, your parents' commutes to work. Find some **friendly families to join you in a car-pool rota**, where different people drive on different days and you all share lifts. All it takes is a bit of organization, and everyone in your Car Pool Posse will reduce their emissions and their fuel bills. As an extra incentive, add this rule: take turns for everyone to put on their **Car Pool Posse Playlist** to liven up the journey.

*Using public transport like trains and buses rather than cars is also good for reducing your travel emissions on shorter, local journeys too.

76
HAVE A HOOT AT NIGHT

It's not just daytime that's good for exploring – there's a whole wonderful world that comes to life after the lights go out. Gather a group together (including an adult) and **think like an owl** by going on a **night safari** in the woods.

Pick a route that's safe – good paths, and away from steep drops. You'll need to take torches (head torches are ideal), wrap up well, and bring refreshments. Give yourself a few moments to tune in your night-time senses before you start walking. If the moon is bright enough, switch your torches off and let your eyes get used to the dark – after a minute or two your night vision should kick in.

If it's a *really* dark night, find a good place to stop for a while, dim the lights, and let the woods come to life around you. Keep silent and still, and listen out for noises: flutters, scuttles, rustles, squeaks, hoots, grunts and growls are all clues. You might even see pairs of eyes peeping back at you. Use your **expert knowledge** (see **3**) to identify as many creatures of the night as you can. Who knows, you might even encounter some of the stars of your night-time wildlife cam (see **56**).

If going on a night safari (see **76**) has left you wanting more midnight adventures, try **sleeping beneath the stars** by going camping in a 'dark skies' area. These are usually wide-open parts of countryside or parkland where there is little or no light pollution from buildings, traffic or people. Before you go, look at the weather forecast and pick a clear night, ideally when it's a new moon as the brightness of a full moon makes stars harder to see.

77
WONDERING STARS

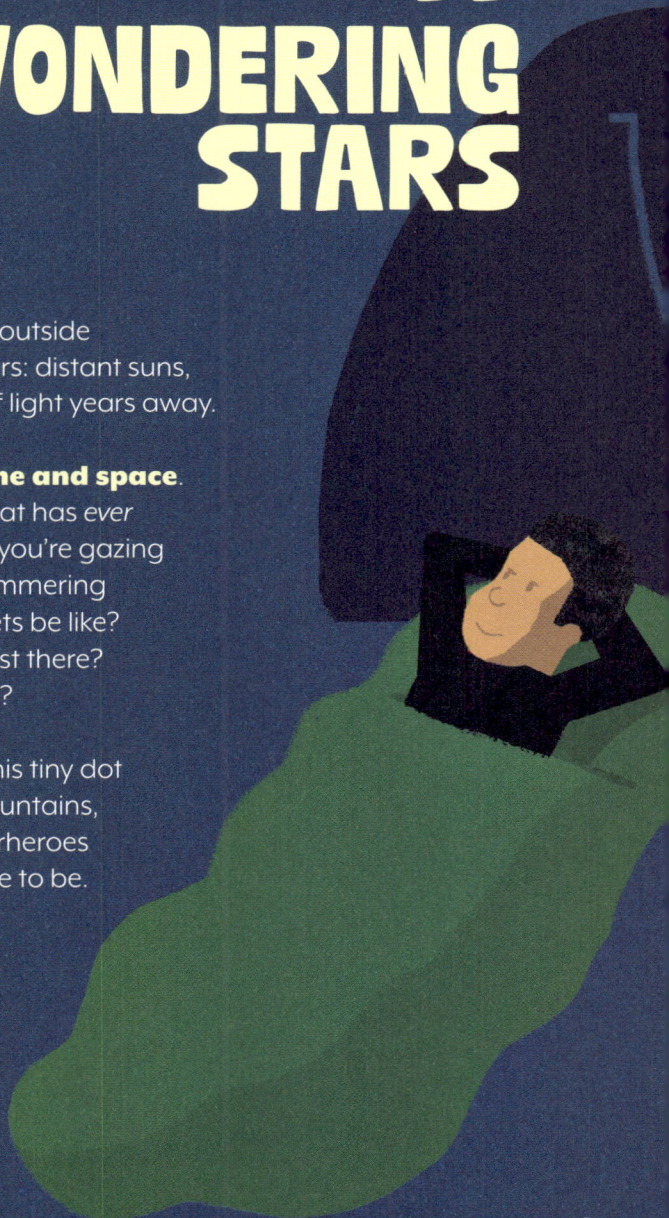

You don't have to sleep outside *all* night; after all, you can't see the stars while your eyes are shut. But you *can* lie outside your tent for a while and just... gaze. What do you see? Stars: distant suns, planets, solar systems, galaxies, thousands and millions of light years away.

Let your imagination take you on a **journey through time and space**. Start with this thought: *every* human and *every* creature that has *ever* lived on Planet Earth has looked up at the same stars that you're gazing at right now. Now imagine there's life on some of these shimmering specks. What might the different, yet-to-be-explored planets be like? What sort of landscapes, habitats and creatures could exist there? Or are they all empty, apart from the planet that you're on?

Then think **how lucky we are to live on our planet** – this tiny dot on someone else's horizon, but alive with forests, lakes, mountains, oceans, deserts, beaches, birds, fish, creatures... and superheroes like you, who make this star of all stars an even better place to be.

Finally, when your eyelids are starting to droop, crawl back inside your tent, and drift off with a happy glow to dreams of galaxies, planets, worlds, Earth, nature, and... stars. Maybe you *can* see them with your eyes closed after all...

Bricks – for keeping homes
dry and off the ground

Bamboo canes

Untreated wood planks,
or recycled wooden
crates and pallets

Moss

Logs with
holes drilled

Facing sunlight

Include lots of gaps to
enable maintenance

Build off the ground

78
BUILD A
BUG-FRIENDLY
BOROUGH

Modern life is tough on bugs and minibeasts – overly manicured gardens and artificial grass, pesticides and insecticides, concreted drives and patios, and ever-decreasing wild areas all threaten insect habitats. But a little eco-planning can make a huge difference to the bug population in your patch. And when the bugs bounce back, so too does other wildlife – everything from flowers and fruit to mammals and birds will begin to flourish. To go with activities like Make a Magic Pond (see **8**) and Let the Grass Grow (see **6**), you can also do a bit of home building to **turn your garden into a thriving bug neighbourhood**.

As well as the design above, many nature organizations offer online tips for constructing big bug hotels, which you can make as basic or as fancy as you like – from motel to five-star, and anywhere in between. As long as there are plenty of gaps, holes and dark spaces for your guests to check in to, your insect visitors will love it. And you can also spread things out with other residences dotted around the garden – your very own bug suburbia – and give different communities space to thrive.

THINGS TO REMEMBER

Like anyone, bugs don't like to have their style cramped, so make sure you don't pack the rooms in too tightly when building your hotel. Also, all good hotels need a regular spruce up. Make sure to clean out or replace any tubes or bamboo canes from time to time, in order to avoid mould and fungus build-up.

Make secure (so it doesn't move in the wind)

Locate near to greenery, such as moss

MORE BUG BOROUGH HABITATS...

Smooth-edged bamboo canes
2⅜–4in (60–100mm) in diameter, and at least 4in (100mm) in length.
GOOD FOR: Solitary bees

Shady rock piles
GOOD FOR: Invertebrates, and even frogs and toads

Log piles, furnished with leaves and vegetation.
GOOD FOR: Beetles, ladybirds, hibernating and breeding insects

Spiders:
Good for plants as they feed on smaller insects, helping to keep balance in ecosystems. And good snacks for birds too.

Ladybirds:
Everyone loves a ladybird – except for aphids, because ladybirds love them.

79
LEARN YOUR MINIBEASTS

Slugs and snails:
Keen munchers who help recycle nutrients into the soil, and also good snacks for birds and critters too.

Bees, butterflies and moths:
Pollinators, essential for helping flowers and plants to grow and spread.

It would be an impossible task to learn about every minibeast species on Earth – around one million types of insect alone have been recorded so far, and it's thought that there could be as many as NINE million more species yet to be discovered. And minibeasts are more than just insects: spiders, millipedes, snails – in fact any invertebrate (a creature without a backbone). The variety of these fascinating creatures that are so important to our ecosystems highlights the amazing diversity of the natural world. There are **tiny ones** and *looooong ones*, **ones with six legs** and **ones with hundreds**, **smooth ones** and **hairy ones**, **ones that jump** and **ones that crawl**, **flying ones** and **swimming ones**, **ones that live for hours** and **ones that live for years**, and even **ones that start off as one thing and end up as another**. But you can start your minibeast expert journey with a simpler challenge: getting to know the common species in your area, and seeing if you can find out about **one type** of **each of the ones** above. Turn your research into your own **Minibeast Spotter's List**, to add to your expert collection.

TRANSFORM A SMALL SPACE

Most people don't have access to huge gardens, fields or meadows in which to carry out big green projects. But there are always things you can do on a small scale in small spaces that can have a big impact on wildlife. And remember, each transformed patio, yard or concrete patch is an extra buzz stop on your local bee wildlife corridor.*

80 PERK UP A PATIO (OR YARD, OR BALCONY)

Planters come in all kinds of shapes and sizes – from large free-standing troughs that turn patios into temporary veg patches, to simple, small boxes for flowers and herbs that can brighten up windowsills. You can buy them from garden centres, or team up with a DIY-loving mum or dad to construct your own. Vegetables that grow well in **free-standing planters** include small potato varieties, carrots, beetroots and broad beans, or you could use one to grow all your different herbs in one place (see **16**). **Window boxes** and hanging baskets are great for planting a mix of smaller and trailing flowers, such as petunias, fuchsias and geraniums. And don't forget little old **plant pots** – even one or two pots with small flowers in makes a difference.

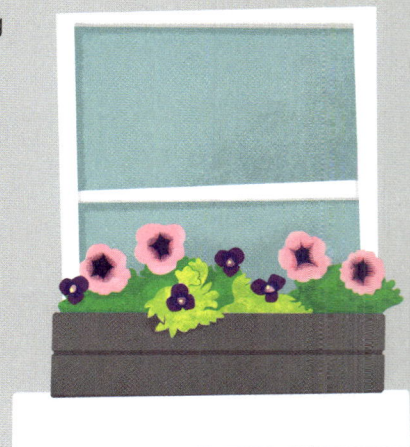

* See **86** and find out about Oslo's Bee Highway!

81 BRING A WALL TO LIFE

Who said gardens always have to be *horizontal*? Growing a *vertical* garden – also known as a **living wall** – is a great way to make the most of limited space. You can do this in a few ways. One is to plant **climbers** – things like clematis, wisteria, ivy, jasmine – at the base of the wall, which will grow quickly upwards and cling to either the wall or a trellis. Another is to attach a **multi-pocket planter** – imagine a dozen trouser pockets in a grid – to your wall, and fill them with lots of small plants that will turn into a green screen. And another is to **hang individual plant pots** high up on your wall and let the leaves and flowers of trailing plants like lobelia, verbena and calibrachoa tumble downwards as they grow.

82 TURN ANYTHING INTO A FLOWER POT

Here's a fun challenge for you and your Green Gang: see who can **make a flower planter out of the most unusual re-used object**. Wellies, wheelbarrows, watering cans, worn-out suitcases, broken kettles, biscuit tins, egg boxes, ex-boxes, shells of old X-Boxes... anything goes! The planters can be for indoor or outdoor use, and the only rule is that your repurposed planter product has to be brimming with lovely, colourful flowers when it's finished. You could even turn the challenge into a community-wide competition to help transform nature-less areas into planter-filled paradises (and Bee Highway buzz stops).

83 MAKE A MINI-POND

Just like a Magic Pond will make wildlife appear (see **8**), so too will a mini-pond. You can sink it into a hole in the lawn, but you can also have it freestanding in your yard or on your patio. Then, simply... leave it, and wait for the wildlife to arrive. **All you need is:**

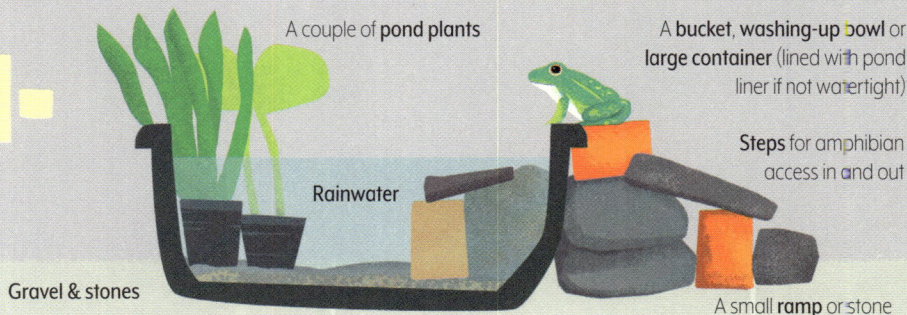

A couple of **pond plants**

A **bucket**, **washing-up bowl** or **large container** (lined with pond liner if not watertight)

Rainwater

Steps for amphibian access in and out

Gravel & stones

A small **ramp** or stone

5, **11**, **15**, **16** & **38** will all help your small space transformation.

The handy thing about trees is that they give you incredibly useful takeaway clues to help you identify them: their leaves.

You can start your journey into learning your trees by **collecting fallen leaves** on your walks, bringing them home, and using an online leaf identifier to figure out what sort of tree they came from.

Once you know that, find out some more facts about the tree in question, and add them to a **Tree Expert notebook**: bark colour, height, spread, blossom colour, seed size and shape, where it tends to grow, deciduous or evergreen. And don't forget the most fun part of making your notes: **take leaf rubbings** to illustrate them by laying a page on top of the leaf and colouring over the paper with the side of a crayon until a replica of the leaf appears.

Every time you find a new type of leaf, that's another type of tree you can add to your **Tree Expert** knowledge bank.

84
LEARN YOUR TREES

Mango tree

Gingko tree

Rubber tree

Rubber tree

Beech tree

Red maple tree

Japanese yew tree

Willow tree

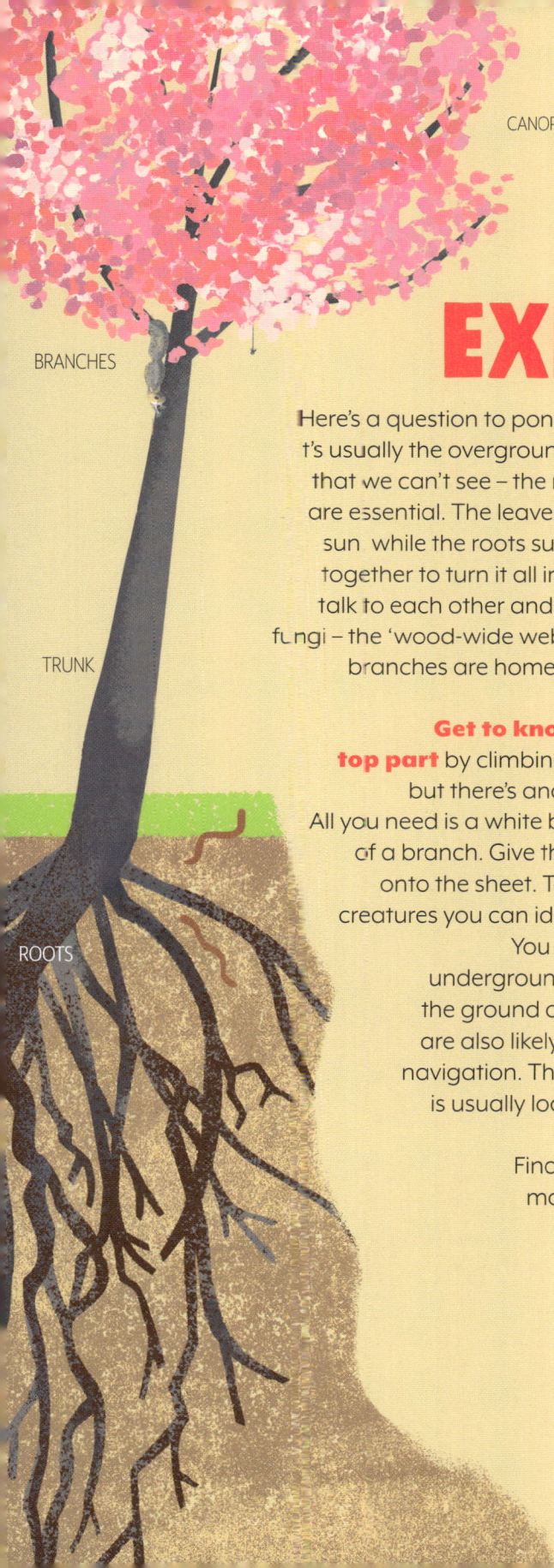

CANOPY

BRANCHES

TRUNK

ROOTS

85
EXPLORE A TREE

Here's a question to ponder. Which way is up for a tree? When we think of a tree it's usually the overground part that we picture. But there's a whole lot more tree that we can't see – the roots, spreading outwards and downwards. Both parts are essential. The leaves absorb carbon dioxide from the air and light from the sun while the roots supply water from the ground – and the whole tree works together to turn it all into energy and release oxygen. That's not all. Trees also talk to each other and share energy via their roots, with the aid of networks of fungi – the 'wood-wide web'. And trees are not solitary above ground either – their branches are home to countless birds, bugs and mammals, all co-existing.

Get to know a tree from top to bottom. You can **explore the top part** by climbing it (safely), or building a tree house (even more safely), but there's another way to investigate it with your feet on the ground. All you need is a white bed sheet. Place it underneath the canopy, within reach of a branch. Give that branch a gentle shake and see what minibeasts fall onto the sheet. Take a photo, then after you've returned them, see what creatures you can identify. **Exploring the bottom part** of a tree is trickier. You might see roots sticking out of a riverbank or hillside, or underground. But you can also trace roots on the surface: ridges in the ground often indicate tree roots just below, and clusters of fungi are also likely to be growing above roots. You can even use roots for navigation. The thickest root that sticks out from the base of the trunk is usually located on the side where the strongest winds blow from.

Finally, **draw an overground-underground picture** or map of your garden, street or nearest park. Include all the parts of the tree, and how far you imagine the roots of the wood-wide web spread beneath the surface.

Your Family Tree could be perfect for exploration – see **23**.

86 WILDLIFE CORRIDOR

A long time ago, animals could roam freely across the land. Then came humans, farmland, roads and cities, leaving natural habitats divided and isolated, making it much harder for wildlife to interact and flourish. **Creating wild corridors** that let creatures move safely between green spaces is a really important way of helping nature, and increasing population numbers. The simplest way to make your patch part of a wildlife corridor is to ensure animals can get in and out of your garden.

Hedges are the best garden barriers – they are also really important habitats for birds and mammals – but if your garden does have a fence or wall around it, there are a couple of easy solutions. If you have a fence, ask a parent to cut a small hole in the bottom (check with your neighbour first), or dig a hole underneath it. For gardens with walls, plant climbers that will grow quickly up them, and which act as a natural ladder for little critters (see **81**).

Ask your neighbours if *they'll* do the same on the other side – and if *they* ask *their* other neighbour too, you'll quickly have a wildlife corridor that stretches as long as your street. If you don't have your own garden (or even if you do) you could ask your school or community to campaign for the creation of a wildlife corridor that covers the whole neighbourhood (see **94**).

INSPIRATIONAL INTERNATIONAL CORRIDORS

Check out some of these big wildlife corridor projects to spark some ideas:

Oslo's Bee Highway
A pollinator passage of flowers, green rooftops, wild patches, bug hotels and beehives that helps bees travel across Norway's capital city.

European Green Belt
A natural corridor that connects important wild areas from Finland in Northern Europe to Greece in Southern Europe.

Jaguar Corridor Initiative
A project that aims to create a safe passageway for jaguars to roam all the way from Mexico to Argentina.

Great Green Wall
A plan to make a 4,400 mile (7,000km) green corridor across Saharan Africa, running through 11 different countries.

87
MAKE A WILD MAP

This is another 'year apart' challenge. Start by **drawing a map** of your neighbourhood on a large sheet of paper, with your house in the middle. Put as much **green** detail on it as possible: all the gardens, parks, school fields, verges and trees that are there now. But only use a *light shade* to represent the green spaces that are not really wild... yet: things like short lawns and verges, gardens that are isolated by walls and fences, patches that could do with a nature-friendly makeover.

Then, as you complete more and more of the activities in the book, **draw a new map**. Use a **bright, bold green** to add in all the spaces and places in your area that have become more wild since you made the first map. Your garden, yard or balcony; your Green Gang members' gardens, yards or balconies; your school growing projects, wildlife corridors, longer verges, new trees, wildflower areas, windowsills, new birdhouses, new ponds, community vegetable plots, Sprinkle Sortie sites, and anything else that's greener and wilder than when you started your Superhero journey.

88
BECOME AN ECO-RANGER

Using your wildlife map (see **87**) as a base, plan and plot a **local walking safari route** that takes in as much interesting local nature as possible. Use your 'Expert Knowledge' to add details on the birds, minibeasts, mammals and trees that populate your area, and where and when the best places, seasons and times are to spot them. You can then raise money for your Big Wild Project (see **94**) by selling copies of your self-guided eco tour, or organize a big community or school nature safari walk with you as the **eco-ranger guide**.

89
POLLEN POWER-UP

If you've already built a bug hotel (see **78**), **planting a wildflower patch** is like adding a top-notch restaurant to the area: an all-you-can-eat flowering feast of nectar and pollen that makes your neighbourhood the place to be for bees, butterflies and all kinds of other flying pollinators.*

The preparation and maintenance of a wildflower patch is fairly straightforward. **Wildflower seed packs** are readily available, and the most important thing is to select a mix that is native to your area. Sow your seeds in autumn to see the best, and earliest, results the following summer, although you can also plant in spring. Clear the area you want to transform down to a thin layer of top soil, and scatter around ⅕oz (5g) of seeds per 11 square feet (1 square metre). And that's it – it won't be long until your garden is transformed into a flowery, species-rich wildlife haven, and the **most desirable area for any bug** to move into.

90
SPRINKLE SORTIES

This is a fun mission for you and your Green Gang to try. Stock up from your Super Seed Superstore (see **38**), and embark on some **sprinkling sorties around your neighbourhood**. Packet up some seeds in envelopes, add a little 'please plant me' note, and deliver them throughout the neighbourhood.

Alternatively, you could take a little bag or pocket full of seeds when you go on a walk, and sprinkle them in public grassy areas that look like they could do with a bit of a wild boost (check with your council first if they allow this). Your seeds might grow, they might not; they might blow, they might not; and they might get mowed (but they might not). Then enjoy keeping an eye out on your walks over the coming weeks and months, and see if your seeds begin to bloom.

*If you don't have garden space, you can fill your planters (see **80**), with wildflower seed mix or use it on your Sprinkle Sorties.

91
FEED YOUR FLOWERS

There's a simple trick to give your wildflowers (and anything else you're growing) a boost – **converting your leftover food into compost**. It's important to avoid food waste as much as possible (see The Big Cook, **43–46**), but when you do end up with unusable leftovers, turning them into flower fertilizer is a great option.

Good things to compost include scraps like veg peel, fruit rinds, bread, eggshells, tea bags, and coffee grounds – but not meat or cooked food. Different gardeners use different composting methods, but the easiest is to dig a series of small holes, one at a time, along your wildflower bed or in your veg patch, fill them with chopped up leftovers, top with a few leaves (see **31**), and cover back over. The microbes in the soil, and probably a few worms, will quickly get to work breaking it all down and turning it into nutrients to help new things grow.

92
VERDANT VERGES

The strips of grass between roads and pavements, in the centre of roundabouts, and along the middle of highways are perfect patches for giving the urban jungle a green boost. But there's a problem. Often, just as the grass begins to grow tall enough for the dandelions, daisies and other wildflowers to flourish, and the bees and bugs to arrive, along comes a fleet of mowers to cut it all back and keep the verges short and flowerless.

PLEASE DON'T MOW ME!

THINGS YOU CAN DO TO HELP INCLUDE:

- Make a little 'Please Don't Mow Me' sign to stick in the verge nearest your house.

- Ask your school if they can let all the verges in and around the buildings grow long in the spring and summer.

- Talk to the neighbours on your street about signing a letter to your town council asking to use your street as a 'no-mow' trial zone.

- Include safely accessible pavement verges on your Sprinkle Sortie route, and scatter some wildflower seeds.

- Search online to see if there any 'wild verge' campaigns run by environmental organizations in your area, and find out what you can do to get involved.

- See if your school can find a local business to sponsor a wildflower roundabout (see **94**).

93 LEARN YOUR MAMMALS

Your final **Become An Expert** challenge might seem easy. After all, most people already know what a mouse looks like, or the difference between a fox and a badger. But could you tell a dormouse from a field mouse, if you caught a glimpse of one in the long grass? How about a weasel or an otter from a ferret or a stoat if something long and furry flashed by in a field? A common pipistrelle from a soprano pipistrelle if a bat posed for a portrait on your wildlife camera (see **56**)? Or a vole from a mole if something popped up out of a hole?

Start by **choosing one category**: rodents, mustelids (your weaselly type creatures), or bats, for example. Find out as much as you can about **five different species**: their size, colour, distinctive fur patterns, male and female differences, habitat, diet, footprints, droppings (see **54**). Jot your research down in your expert notebook. Try to memorize your facts. Ask a friend to quiz you until you get full marks. Then, try learning five more species from another category, and keep going until you become a **true mammal mastermind**.

Now you're a mammal expert, take on the other expert challenges – see **3**

94 BIG WILD PROJECT

This is definitely a challenging challenge: come up with an idea for a **BIG WILD PROJECT**, and make it happen. It may sound a bit scary, but have no fear. Put on your **Green Superhero cape**, be bold, brave, and take a leap into the unknown. It might work out, or it might not, but the important thing is to try.

Your aim is to transform somewhere in your neighbourhood into a **brilliant**, **blooming**, **new wild space**, using some of the techniques you've learnt along your superhero journey. Scout out a good location (your Wild Map might be useful here – see **87**), and then ask for permission to start your project. It could be a public place, an abandoned car park, a corner of your school grounds or even the middle of a roundabout (see **92**). You'll certainly need help to make this happen – parents, friends, neighbours, school, your Green Gang – but the more people you can get involved, the better. Remember: you might be the Green Superhero, but you're not alone on your planet-saving quest.

HOUSE FOR A MOUSE

Small mammals looking for somewhere to hibernate over winter are usually most grateful if you rake up a mound of leaves in a corner of your garden. Small wooden boxes with narrow entrances are usually appealing too – different animals need different sized and located boxes, so research the best option for the type you'd like to attract.

SEEK A SPONSOR

You could also ask any adults you know if the company they work for might be interested in sponsoring your Big Wild Project – they give you some money to carry out the wilding work, in return for some good, positive advertising. This is happening more and more on a big scale with businesses and environmental projects, so there's no reason why local companies shouldn't want to do the same. And if one company does it, it might encourage others to do the same.

Please don't mow me

95 MIDNIGHT MOTH SAFARI

Spotting wildlife at night is not easy – that's why many creatures decide to do their foraging and feeding under cover of darkness, after all. But there's a neat trick you can use to get a good glimpse of one well-known nocturnal worker: **moths**. All you need is a washing line, a torch, a dark night, and a white sheet (the same one you use for your Explore-a-Tree Investigation will do nicely – see **85**).

Hang the sheet over the washing line, and turn off any nearby lights – apart from your torch, which you can shine directly on to the sheet. Before long, a curious cast of moths of all shapes, sizes and shades should appear, magnetically drawn to your dazzling light show. If you can, take a photo of the moths, and use an online identifier to see how many different types you can recognize. When you've finished, switch your torch off and allow the moths to fly away safely before you take the sheet down.

Like bees and butterflies, moths are really important pollinators. After you've done your first Midnight Moth Safari, try planting some more moth-friendly flowers like evening primrose, honeysuckle and buddleia, and then re-doing it to see how many more magnificent moths have moved into your patch.

Sometimes it can seem impossible to think about saving the *whole planet* when there are almost 200 countries in the world, each with their own environmental challenges. Too dry, too wet, too much traffic, poverty, pollution, deforestation, every country has its own difficulties to overcome. But there's a saying that goes: **'a problem shared is a problem halved'**. So... what if all the knowledge and expertise that you've developed on your Green Superhero quest could be helpful to potential Green Superheroes in another country?

A great way to share ideas and inspiration is for your school to become officially **twinned with a school from another country**. Ask your teacher if your class or school can find an international partner – you could even suggest the country*

You can talk with your twin about each other's green challenges and solutions, swap ideas about the nature projects you're both involved with, and even help with campaigning and raising money to support each other's actions. Sharing the Green Superhero positivity means each partner's problems become a little less difficult to tackle. And if everyone who reads this book gets *their* school to find a twin from a different country, that's an awful lot of problems halved all across the planet.

96
HALVE A PROBLEM

*International organizations like the British Council have twinning schemes that your school can sign up to.

97
MAKE A MINI-BIOSPHERE

While your Green Superhero ideas spread out into a different part of the world (see **95**), you can also recreate a different part of the world at home by **making a mini-biosphere**. The big definition of the word biosphere is all the places on Earth where life and ecosystems exist – and a mini-biosphere is an ecosystem that exists inside a contained space, complete with its own micro-climate.

Mini-biospheres are a fascinating way to see how life thrives when the environment is well balanced and all living things are working in harmony with each other. All you need to make your own miniature-world is a **glass jar**, **bottle or bowl**, **some little stones**, **soil** and **small plants**. Choose plants that belong together in the type of ecosystem you want to create – for example, cacti and succulents for a desert world, or ferns and mosses for a tropical one – and add an appropriate amount of water, before sealing the container. **Your world** should then take care of itself – oxygen, carbon dioxide and water will all be produced and recycled by the occupants of your mini ecosystem. You could even try to recreate the climate native to your twinned school (see **96**), and they could replicate yours, so that you get even more of a connection of each other's environment.

Sealable jar or glass bowl

Plants

Moss

Add some rainwater

Soil

Small stones/pebbles

98
DESIGN A GREEN CITY

Imagine it's your job to create a brand new city. What would you include to make sure it was a green place to live? Use whatever you like to come up with a **design for a futuristic sustainable city**: Minecraft, Lego, the contents of your recycling bin, or simply paper and pens to make a town plan or a poster.

Think about everything you've done on your quest to become a Green Superhero, and how you might use all that new knowledge to combine nature with city life to make it the best of both worlds. Take a picture of it when you've finished, and include it in your letter to a leader (see **100**). You never know, you might just have had a **brilliant idea** that could change how people of the future live...

99
GET PHILOSOPHICAL

Different parts of the world have different philosophies that reflect something positive about living there: an attitude to life, a way to be happy, less stressed, more helpful, connected with nature and a part of making that community a good place to be.

You've already discovered the Norwegian philosophy of friluftsliv (see **66**), which involves making a commitment to spend time doing things in the outdoors, whatever the weather. **Come up with a slogan and a philosophy** that represents a good, natural way *you'd* like to live life. It might become the motto for your Sustainable City (see **98**), your school, your family, your Green Gang (see **47**), or just... you. You could make badges or posters with your slogan on – or simply use it as your private philosophy to remind you how *you'd* like to live your best, greenest life.

MORE GREAT PHILOSOPHIES

JOIE DE VIVRE
'The joy of living'. In Canada it has an extra meaning: embracing the joy and adventure of outdoor life

PURA VIDA
The pure or simple life. The Costa Rican idea of focusing on what's important in life, such as friends, family, food and laughter, and making time to enjoy nature.

XING FU
From China – it means to live a good life that is sufficient, sustainable and has meaning.

LAGOM
Not too much, not too little, but just enough. This Swedish philosophy has a double meaning – don't take or use more things than you need, and also have a good balance between work and enjoying life.

100
WRITE
A LETTER

FROM THE DESK OF

When you're young, there's always someone older who seems to be in charge: parents, teachers, mayors, politicians... They make *all* the decisions about important things (and sometimes they don't always all seem to be good decisions).

Now think about this. When you're older, someone who's *the same age now* as you will be making the important decisions about the way we look after the planet. Why shouldn't it be **you**? It can be a bit scary to stand up and make your voice heard. Other people might be louder, or more confident, and not everyone might agree with what you have to say. But be brave—remember, you now have super-powers, and this is your last, two part step to becoming a fully fledged hero.

PART ONE

Try to make a first, small step to getting involved in decision making on a local level. It could be joining the school council, starting a nature group, or simply speaking with your teacher or parents about the green issues that concern you, and any ideas you have about what to do about them.

PART TWO

THINK BIG. **Write a letter to the leader of the country or city that you live in**. Tell them about your quest to become a Green Superhero. About the things you've done to help nature in your area. About the way you've teamed up with others to make your community greener. About your ideas: your pedal power invention, your green philosophy, your sustainable city, your green laws. And, finally, tell them about something practical and positive you'd love your leader to do to help the planet. Sign it, send it, and sit back (with a Superhero Smoothie) knowing that **your voice is going to be heard**.

One more thing. Don't forget to colour in the last bit of your Green Superhero Footprint that you drew way back when you first started reading this book – see **1**.

CONGRATULATIONS, YOU'RE A GREEN SUPERHERO!

RESOURCES & TIPS

Some great organizations and useful websites to help you on your Green Superhero journey

ORGANIZATIONS

WWF
An international charity helping wildlife and nature across the world.

wwf.panda.org

REWILDING EUROPE
An organization that works to restore and create new wilderness areas.

rewildingeurope.com

SEEK
A new app by to help identify trees and plants.

inaturalist.org

ACTIVITY-SPECIFIC

1 YOUR GREEN SUPERHERO FOOTPRINT
An environmental footprint calculator:
- footprint.wwf.org.uk

4 YEAR OF THE BIRD
Big birdwatch surveys:
- RSPB – rspb.org.uk
- Great Backyard Bird Count – birdcount.org

10 LEARN ABOUT LABELS
Sustainability logos:
- Fairtrade – fairtrade.org.uk
- Rainforest Alliance – rainforest-alliance.org
- Marine Stewardship Council – msc.org

NATIONAL PARKS AROUND THE WORLD

Incredible outdoor places to explore. Here are some to get you started:

UK
nationalparks.uk/parks

CANADA
parks.canada.ca/pn-np

USA
nps.gov

JAPAN
japan.travel/national-parks

AUSTRALIA
parksaustralia.gov.au

EUROPE
nationalparksofeurope.com

12 BRUSH WITH BAMBOO
More about bamboo:
- worldbamboo.net

14-17 GROWN YOUR OWN
Great growing ideas and tips:
- Royal Horticultural Society – rhs.org.uk
- American Horticultural Society – ahsgardening.org

22 MAKE A NATURE DOCUMENTARY
Some cool nature programmes to check out:
- BBC – Planet Earth, Blue Planet, Frozen Planet
- National Geographic – Arctic Tale, March of the Penguins
- Disney – Nature: Earth and Oceans
- Netflix – Wild Babies, Great Barrier Reef

ABOUT THE AUTHORS

TOM

Tom is an author and scriptwriter, based in Yorkshire, UK. He's written about nature and exploring from all corners of the globe, as well as his own back yard of the Peak District, and he's worked with some very cool outdoor organisations including National Parks UK, Rough Guide, National Geographic, and Explorer HQ. He also writes for some of the most popular children's and adult TV shows, from adventuring animation Go Jetters to the quiz classic Mastermind, and for comedy and factual podcasts and audio programmes. When he's not writing, he loves getting out and about on his mountain bike, and playing the brilliant Swedish game of Kubb – also known as Viking chess (give it a go, you'll love it!).

JOSH

Joshua Rice is an illustrator and designer based in London, UK. His graphic, colourful work has been shortlisted for industry awards, exhibited in the London Transport Museum and featured by clients and collaborators such as National Parks UK, Historic Royal Palaces and Explorer HQ. Originally from Ontario, Canada, he trained as a historian before moving to the UK almost twenty years ago. Today, he works on art and other things from his home studio in Ealing, west London, where he lives with his family.

ACKNOWLEDGEMENTS

Tom's: Thanks to Hannah, Sam and Lucy, and to the generations of the Thomas family for inspiring and sharing a lifelong love of nature and the outdoors; to Josh for his inspirational art, and to Mark Pearce at Explorer HQ for sparking this creative collaboration; to Jonathan and Susie at GMC for their encouragement and support for this book. And finally, the biggest thanks go to you – the Green Superheroes – for taking care of our amazing planet.

Josh's: Thank you to all who helped inspire, realise and make this book possible, especially Tom, Mark, Jonathan, Susie, Celia, Ormond, Albert and Sox.

First published in 2024 by Button Books, an imprint of Guild of Master Craftsman Publications Ltd
Castle Place, 166 High Street, Lewes,
East Sussex BN7 1XU, UK

Text © Tom Jordan, 2024
Illustrations © Joshua Rice, 2024
Copyright in the Work © GMC Publications Ltd, 2024

ISBN 978 1 78708 156 7

Distributed by Publishers Group West in the United States.

All rights reserved

The right of Tom Jordan to be identified as the author of this work has been asserted in accordance with the Copyright, Designs and Patents Act 1988, sections 77 and 78.

No part of this publication may be reproduced, stored in a retrieval system, or transmitted in any form or by any means without the prior permission of the publisher and copyright owner.

While every effort has been made to obtain permission from the copyright holders for all material used in this book, the publishers will be pleased to hear from anyone who has not been appropriately acknowledged and to make the correction in future reprints.

The publishers and author can accept no legal responsibility for any consequences arising from the application of information, advice, or instructions given in this publication.

A catalog record for this book is available from the British Library.

Publisher Jonathan Bailey
Production Jim Bulley
Senior Project Editor Susie Behar
Design Manager Robin Shields
Design & Illustration Joshua Rice
Colour origination by GMC Reprographics
Printed and bound in China

For more on Button Books, contact:

GMC Publications Ltd,
Castle Place,
166 High Street,
Lewes, East Sussex,
BN7 1XU, United Kingdom
Tel: +44 (0)1273 488005
buttonbooks.co.uk
buttonbooks.us

Transform a small space – see **80**